Documentary Television in Canada

Documentary Television in Canada

From National Public Service to Global Marketplace

DAVID HOGARTH

McGill-Queen's University Press
Montreal & Kingston · London · Ithaca

© McGill-Queen's University Press 2002
ISBN 0-7735-2339-1

Legal deposit second quarter 2002
Bibliothèque nationale du Québec

Printed in Canada on acid-free paper that is 100%
ancient forest free (100% post-consumer recycled),
processed chlorine free, and printed with vegetable-
based, low VOC inks.

This book has been published with the help of a grant
from the Humanities and Social Sciences Federation
of Canada, using funds provided by the Social
Sciences and Humanities Research Council of
Canada.

McGill-Queen's University Press acknowledges the
financial support of the Government of Canada
through the Book Publishing Industry Development
Program (BPIDP) for its publishing activities. We also
acknowledge the support of the Canada Council
for the Arts for our publishing program.

**National Library of Canada Cataloguing
in Publication Data**

Hogarth, David, 1959–
    Documentary television in Canada : from national
    public service to global marketplace
    Includes bibliographical references and index.
    ISBN 0-7735-2339-1
    1. Documentary television programs – Canada –
    History and criticism. I. Title.
    PN1992.8.D6H63 2001   070.1'95'0971
    C2001-902846-6

Typeset in Sabon 10.5/13
by Caractéra inc., Quebec City

Contents

Preface

This book began as a teaching assignment when I was asked to direct a course on documentary television at Montreal's Concordia University. At the time I had never really considered the differences between documentary television and film, and as I began to assemble the course kit, I realized that many of my colleagues had failed to make the distinction as well. This is particularly true in Canada, where the documentary cinema tradition has been so entrenched in both production and academic circles. Yet the more I thought about it, and the more I watched the programs themselves, I became convinced that a new book on documentaries had to be written in Canada – if only because most documentaries are no longer seen on film, and most are no longer, strictly speaking, "Canadian." This book is thus designed to say something about documentaries and the way they have become increasingly televisual and global in the contemporary era.

I would like to thank a number of people for their help in this project: James Jervis for his intellectual and moral support, Roy Harris and Michelle Melady at CBC Archives for their help in tracking down some of the shows, and my extended family in Toronto and Ottawa. Thanks most of all to my wife, Brigitte. The mistakes, of course, are all mine.

David Hogarth
Toronto
1 May 2000

Documentary Television in Canada

1 Introduction: A Defining Genre

"With regard to television, Canadians cannot afford to daydream," wrote critic Stephen Plumb on the eve of Canada's first domestic telecast in November 1952.[1] Plumb's rather axiomatic argument is by now familiar in Canadian cultural criticism: Every modern nation, he insists, must maintain not only its geographic borders but a sovereign televisual space. In this space the life of the nation must be represented "faithfully and without illusions" so that viewers can develop into full-fledged citizens "with a sense of where they are." Only with documentary realism firmly established as a principle of telecasting can the nation's cultural project "proceed in a modern age."[2] For Plumb, Canadian television is quite simply bound by a documentary imperative.

Documentary television has always held a special fascination for Canada's cultural nationalists. For former CBC executive vice-president Eugene Hallman, programs documenting Canadian life were television's "most unique [cultural] achievement in terms of artistic, technological and and geographic scope."[3] For critic Morris Wolfe, Canada's documentary programs were an "oasis in a [North American] TV wasteland" – a wasteland of "beautiful lies," as he put it.[4] For the officials of the Canadian Television Fund, documentary television remained in 1999 "a profoundly Canadian form" allowing "Canadians to experience the country from coast to coast."[5] Over time, then, and from a number sites for the production and regulation of Canadian culture, documentary programming has been held up by producers, pundits, and policy-makers as Canadian television at its best and most important: that is, Canada's most distinguished contribution to televisual form, and television's most substantial contribution to a Canadian sense of place.[6]

Yet there is another way of thinking about documentary television, a way that has become increasingly prominent in Canada in recent years. Television documentaries are also cultural commodities, *exportable* goods that can be bought, sold, and traded for the profit of producers, distributors, and broadcasters. As *Playback* magazine put it in a recent issue, television documentaries may be significant forms of national self-expression but they are are also "hot properties" with a transnational-commercial as well as a national-cultural dimension.[7] Documentary programs, in this view, have a future beyond the national public service age, in the global cultural markets of the twenty-first century.

This book considers the place and importance of documentary television in Canada, taking into account both these aesthetic-cultural and industrial aspects. Documentary programming, I argue, has been used by a number of Canadian cultural authorities and institutions to define and legitimate both public service and market models of television broadcasting in Canada. At the same time, the genre has served to uphold or resolve distinctions made in Canadian cultural discourse between "quality" and "commercial" television, between the "public" and the "popular," and between the "national" and the "foreign." This, then, is the story of a *defining* genre of Canadian television, a story that tells us a great deal about Canadian television over time, about where it has been and where it might be going as Canada attempts to make the transition to a global cultural economy.

DOCUMENTARY AND PUBLIC SERVICE TELEVISION IN CANADA

How, first of all, has documentary programming helped define Canadian *public service television*? Of course, documentary realism never shaped that medium the way it did Canadian cinema; public service broadcasting was, after all, generally conceived as a comprehensive service in Canada, designed to provide fictional as well as factual programming for all types of (officially recognized) tastes.

But if Canadian television itself was never seriously promoted as a purely documentary vehicle, a case can still be made that documentary programming shaped the way the medium was thought of and used in Canada in a number of decisive ways.

Most basically, documentary shaped the *technologies* of Canadian television – that is, the way its sounds and images were technically produced and processed over time. Documentary radio producers in the 1930s conducted early experiments in sound effects, while wartime documentary technicians in the next decade developed key innovations in actuality recording.[8] Magazine documentaries introduced a "graphic revolution" to Canadian television in the the 1950s,[9] and public affairs documentaries, according to Warner Troyer, "revolutionized" the medium's film and videotape practices in the years that followed.[10] All the while, documentary programs marked a number of significant moments in Canadian broadcast history. Documentary programming formed the core of the Canadian Broadcasting Corporation's first experimental TV transmission in April 1952,[11] its first school broadcast in 1954,[12] and its first colour telecast in 1966.[13] More recently, documentary programs have been used to introduce digital television to the Canadian market.[14]

Just as importantly, documentary programming has shaped Canada's television *aesthetic*. A documentary television aesthetic has arguably been institutionalized in Canada, enshrined in longstanding conventions requiring producers, as critic Penelope Wise once put it, "not to make a show but to find one."[15] This aesthetic has been organizationally sustained by flexible departmental structures encouraging public service producers such as Len Peterson, Joseph Schull, Sidney Newman, Allan King, and Beryl Fox to move back and forth from documentary to drama productions, bringing their techniques with them – for instance, shooting on location or, at a minimum, working hard to duplicate locations to give their shows an "as-found" look. For many producers, documentary television embodies a Canadian public service television aesthetic that eschews the laws of the studio and the marketplace by engaging events in their own time and space, no matter how technically difficult or commercially pointless the project.[16]

Finally, documentary ideals have shaped Canadian television *criticism* and *policy discourse* over time. Canada's social realist TV critics have generally judged fact and fiction programs alike for the "purity" of their reflections of Canadian life, for the "importance" of the issues they have dealt with, and for the merit of the groups they have represented – that is, for their documentary as opposed to dramatic value. John Mistaler's praise of TVOntario's *View from Here* program for its "unflinching portraits of real social problems and marginalized groups" is but one case in point.[17] Formalist critics have similarly commended documentary programs for their stylistic eclecticism and diverse modes of address; Gail Henley, for instance, singled out the CBC's *For the Record* for its demanding and open-ended narrative texts.[18] Canadian critics on all sides of the fence have thus idealized documentary programs as much as fictional shows and more than newscasts in these regards, viewing them as extended and aesthetically flexible sites for the elaboration of cultural meanings.[19] For many, documentary programming embodies everything television could be in Canada.

Canadian broadcast policies reflect a similar broad support for documentary programming. The Massey Commission, which in 1952 presided over the introduction of Canadian television, praised broadcast documentaries for their "reproduction of real as opposed to synthetic situations" and for their formal and textual eclecticism which, true to a public service mandate, satisfied the "interest of minorities" while "developing new tastes among a larger audience."[20] More than three decades later the 1986 Caplan-Sauvageau Report commended documentary programming as a democratic and potentially artistic form, indispensable on both counts to the public service schedule.[21] In both critical and policy discourse, then, documentary television has been held up as quality Canadian broadcasting, faithfully and creatively *representing* Canadians and the real conditions in which they live, while formally *empowering* them by engaging the civic and aesthetic skills they need to participate in cultural affairs. Over time, Canadian television has thus been charged with the task of documenting – and thereby defending – Canadian life.

That said, not all observers consider the documentary television project to be a good thing. Dissenting views are particularly well represented in the academic community. Mary Jane Miller considers anthology drama to be more appropriate to the accomplishment of the CBC mandate, though she notes the institutional obstacles in the way of Canadian fictional television and acknowledges docudramas to be one of Canada's "favourite dramatic forms."[22] Richard Collins sees the documentary mandate to be evidence of the stifling influence of European high culture – culture dedicated to pedagogy and the denial of pleasure, an influence, in his view, accounting for the unpopularity of Canadian television.[23] For Seth Feldman the documentary project symptomizes an undeveloped cultural formation still bound by a colonial imperative to name and administer things.[24] For Kevin Dowler the continual demand for Canadians to document and define themselves is evidence of the absence of a civil society capable of constructing its own self-representations without massive bureaucratic intervention.[25] But whatever their various misgivings, all these critics would probably (if ruefully) agree with Morris Wolfe's observation that documentary realism has been at the heart of the Canada's national broadcasting project,[26] decisively shaping the form and function of Canadian public service television in its first half century.[27]

DOCUMENTARY AND THE GLOBAL MARKET

It is thus ironic that this defining public service genre, dedicated to national notions of education and representation, should now be one of Canada's fastest-selling cultural exports.[28] In fact, a study of documentary television tells us something not just about public service television in Canada but about the increasingly transnational environment in which Canadian television now operates. Documentary television can serve as a case study of *globalization*, of the transition from national public service to global market television; as such, it allows us to consider both the ways a particular Canadian cultural form has "gone global," and more general questions concerning the future of public service culture – specifically, free speech and the meaningful representation of place – in a global age.

A study of documentary television in Canada allows us to call into question the *periodization* of globalization – that is, conventional understandings of the transnational television market, of the national public service era that preceded it, and the nature of the transition from one period to the other. Globalization, like postmodernization, is seen by many observers to involve a sudden and decisive break with earlier types of political, economic, and cultural practice.[29] A study of a defining genre of the national and global ages of broadcasting in Canada may help us better understand this transition and the nature of the so-called "great divide" between national and post-national culture in the case of television.[30]

Further, such a study allows us to take a closer look at global culture itself. This area has seen much theorizing in recent years, but most of it has been rather abstract and speculative. According to cultural nationalist accounts, globalization involves the elimination of places and public discussions from cultural discourse, with nations and the issues that are important to them essentially vanishing or "blending together" on global television screens.[31] In postmodern accounts, on the other hand, the process is understood as a radical transition – from "national culture," in which meanings and pleasures are contained within fixed liberal-patriarchal boundaries, to "post-national, post-representational" culture, in which sights and sounds are able to engage in a sort of libidinal freeplay.[32] A study of the way a particular type of programming has been produced in one country over a limited period of time allows us to call into question, in a grounded and empirical way, both the adequacy of these models and the notions of a clear-cut divide between modern (national public service) and postmodern (global market) television that underlie them. In short, a case study of documentary television in Canada allows us to reconsider some of the historical and conceptual underpinnings of recent British and American television theory.[33]

For these reasons this book is concerned not just with documentary programming per se but with the wider national public service and global market environments of which it is a part. While designed primarily as a history of a particular genre in a particular place at a particular time, *Documentary Television in Canada*, I hope, says something of broader significance about the institutions and structures that have governed Canadian television over the last half century, and that will continue to govern it in the foreseeable future.

THE FILM STUDIES TAKE ON DOCUMENTARY

Existing research is of little help in addressing these issues. In Canada there has been surprisingly little analysis of documentary programming, let alone of its relation to public service or global market television. Research on Canadian information television has focused mostly on news programming, a genre with its own distinctive set of production rhythms, viewing patterns, and financial, technological, and regulatory constraints.[34] Research on documentary programming as a whole, on the other hand, has been conducted almost entirely from the vantage point of film studies, a body of literature which, though largely unsympathetic (and often uninterested) in documentary television, is worth reviewing in more detail, if only because it remains far and away the dominant academic approach to the genre in terms of volume and influence in Canada.

Though hardly a unified tradition, film studies has been uncompromising from the start in its critical stance towards broadcast documentary. For John Grierson, the first director of Canada's National Film Board, documentary programs were hardly worth critical notice, tending more towards the flatly factual reports of the newsreel than his own "creative treatments of actuality."[35] For Grierson's followers, documentary programs were aesthetically and politically "regressive," offering what the writer Graham Greene once called "frightened ironed out personalities and censored scripts" rather than the formal innovations and genuine social critiques of documentary film.[36] For later film critics, such programs lacked topical substance, diminished like most broadcasting by their preference for everyday domestic subjects over the long-term issues of serious social reportage. Documentary television in Canada featured only "slight inartistic topics of the moment ... of no permanent value," according to film critic Gerald Pratley.[37] All in all, the genre was seen to lack the essential attributes of high culture defended by Canada's more established documentary film authorities.

In its earliest versions the cinematic critique was dictated by the auteurist tendencies of film criticism and its particular distaste for mass culture, as well as by Grierson and his followers' own interests in cultivating documentary film's reputation as an innovative and critical practice. The polemic was probably driven further by the institutional animosity of Film Board staffers for the CBC which, by the mid-1950s had largely eclipsed the NFB as the major site of documentary production in Canada. But beyond these immediate concerns, the film studies critique gained ground and some depth with the emergence of Marxist and Freudian traditions of film criticism in the 1970s and '80s.

Like most criticism in the film-studies tradition, Peter Steven's *Brink of Reality* argues that documentary television has proven itself structurally incapable of representing Canada in an interesting or reliable way.[38] Due to firmly entrenched commercial and political constraints, Steven insists, the genre has tackled only a few subjects (celebrities, nature themes, and politics narrowly defined) in formally pedestrian ways, dominated by the "same gray style since the 1970s."[39] Typically, Steven provides few examples for illustration, with programs such as CBC's *The Journal* serving as foils for his more detailed analysis of documentary film and independent video. For him, documentary television's rare creative moments are largely borrowed and bastardized versions of more interesting work going on outside the broadcasting world.

Magnus Isaacson echoes most of these themes, focusing as well on what he sees to be documentary television's excessive reliance on "regressive realist" modes of representation, which he believes encourage infantile identification and a blind acceptance of dominant social perspectives.[40] In Isaacson's work, documentary television fails to make the grade even as dominant ideology, its subjects and modes of address not so much *struggled over* in a Gramscian sense as *fixed in place* by network rules, legal restrictions, and commercial constraints. Canadian critiques in the Marxist and Freudian film studies traditions have thus generally regarded documentary television as a hegemonic cultural apparatus *par excellence*, functioning to contain the meanings and pleasures of television within strict liberal-bourgeois boundaries.

The critique has been developed with some feminist and post-colonial twists, variously associating the genre with patriarchy (because of the rigid distinction it allegedly makes between public and private life, and because of its gendered adherence to linear realism),[41] with Eurocentrism (because of its denial of silence, ambiguity, and a genuine post-colonial voice),[42] and even with surveillance and governmentality (because of its relentless intrusion into hidden areas of social life.)[43] The list goes on. Documentary television's reputation as film's evil bland twin is well established in Canada.

There are a number of problems with these approaches, and I will focus on just a few. First, and perhaps most obviously, filmic critiques often assume an idealized history of documentary film itself. The idea that documentary film is innovative, engaged, and thus easily contrasted with the anaemic politics and aesthetics of its TV counterpart is, in fact, questionable at best. Recent studies of the Griersonian tradition have suggested that its ethnographic practices were hardly as in-depth, its aesthetic practices hardly as innovative, and its relations with subjects hardly as democratic as the Film Board's defenders have made out. Brian Winston's account of Grierson and his followers' shoddy research practices, their adherence to Hollywood realist aesthetics, and their complicity with state and corporate institutions[44] certainly calls such assumptions into question, especially when coupled with Marchessault's critique of more recent "alternative" cinematic projects at the NFB.[45]

Perhaps more problematically, film studies critiques have presented a largely erroneous account of documentary television itself, particularly with regard to the way in which programs are *produced*. Steven's and Isaacson's view of program departments as Fordist assembly lines of ideas, producing a "mindless digitalized grist," as Isaacson puts it,[46] is overly functionalist, disallowing as it does any struggles over representation. It is also out of date, based on the notion that Canadian broadcasting is entirely closed to independent productions (which has not been the case for over a decade.) In fact a closer look at the way documentary programs have been produced over time, particularly at the CBC, reveals chronic struggles over basic terms of representation – over the boundaries between "fact" and "fiction," "commerce" and "culture," the "public" and the "private," and even "masculine" and "feminine" modes of address – from the earliest days of public service television (see chapter 3) right on through to the age of the specialty channel (see chapter 5). Even in the most rigidly institutionalized years of public service broadcasting (see chapter 4), documentary television production was never rendered as functionally routine as film studies critiques have made out.[47]

Film studies research also offers problematic explanations of television *texts*. Many critiques mix up documentary programs' eclectic range of reality discourses and modes of address, lumping together the hard empirical claims of journalistic reports, for instance, with the "emotional" realism and "postmodern contingent" realisms of daytime magazines and contemporary independent point of view productions (see the analysis of *Shooting Indians* in chapter 5). Such critiques also tend to confuse television's strategies to represent reality with those of documentary film, even though television productions tend to draw upon a much wider semiotic repertoire, while relying more extensively on non-diegetic speech-led interpretations.

Yet these more "transparent" televisual forms may, in some cases, actually distance or discourage viewers from uncritically accepting the "realities" they are seeing on screen.[48] Finally, critiques of television documentary's "regressive realism" generally fail to distinguish between diverse modes of television editing – for instance, continuity editing versus symbolic montage. Some of these modes are less classically realist than others and less ostensibly "objective" than their filmic counterparts. All of this should make us question the conventional view that documentary film is by nature "progressive" and documentary television "ideological."[49]

Lastly, we should be wary of filmic accounts of documentary television's *reception* and *pleasures* – particularly those that take for granted the total identification of television viewers with realist texts. Besides lacking virtually any ethnographic support, such accounts are theoretically and formally implausible, given the frequent disruptions and disjointed modes of address characteristic of most documentary television texts. Ads, disrupted point of view shots, and frequent direct address inserts may in their eclectic flow encourage a form of low-key engagement quite at odds with filmic ideas of spectatorship.[50] In fact, what evidence exists in this area suggests that for some viewers the pleasure of watching documentary programs involves a suspension of belief, and an acknowledged tension between the "real" and "creative" components of the text.[51] Though we should be wary of generalizing even to this degree, it seems probable that some viewers at some times may be watching to "struggle with" rather than "lose themselves in" documentary television texts.

Whatever we make of these research findings, it seems clear that Canadian film studies has so far offered an inadequate account of the power and pleasure of documentary television. This book is designed in part to rescue the genre from the corners of this research, focusing on the ways documentaries in Canada have been produced and distributed in uniquely televisual ways for over half a century. As a genre that has been just as innovative, just as provocative, and almost always more popular than documentary film ever was in Canada, documentary television in Canada is plainly worth another look.

DOCUMENTARY IN TELEVISION TERMS

What exactly are Canadian television documentary programs, and how should we study them? How, for instance, should we distinguish them from documentary films? And how should we categorize them in relation to other types of television? John Corner offers a general working definition based on textual form and viewer expectations that might help us in this respect. Documentary programs, in his view, are those whose primary interest lies in their referentiality, in what they "indicate about the world through sounds and images."[52] This is a broad definition and perhaps a useful starting point, but in the case of Canadian television we encounter immediate conceptual difficulties. Can we assume, for instance, that the interest of vérité shows or reality television programs lies in their referentiality as opposed to their sense of "proximity" to everyday life? And how should we classify "counter-referential" works of producers like Canada's Maya Gallus – works designed to call the referentiality of their own accounts into question?

Similarly, classifying documentary programs according to their visual styles or formal characteristics becomes problematic when we consider the eclectic range of camera shots, lighting styles, audio registers, and editing techniques employed by Canadian productions such as "Schizophrenia" (see the analysis in chapter 3), *Warrendale* (see chapter 4), and *Shooting Indians* (see chapter 5). It is partly because of this stylistic range that confusion over the boundaries of documentary has been so endemic in Canada. As critic Mary Ross noted back in 1965, "for most viewers documentary means just about anything that doesn't carry a storyline or give away prizes"[53] – though as we shall see in chapter 3, documentary shows always carried the former and frequently gave away the latter, even in their earliest years.

Jeremy Tunstall takes a seemingly sounder approach by defining documentary programs according to their production methods. Documentaries, he notes, tend to have longer gestation periods, smaller staffs, and different relations of production than their current-affairs counterparts and are subject to less severe ratings pressures and external supervision.[54] But exceptions to these rules abound in Canada, where documentary production schedules and staffing arrangements vary wildly, from the two-year research schedules and forty-person crews at work on the CBC's *Canada: A People's History* (2000), to the three-person teams and three-week turnaround schedules typical of many specialty channel documentaries. One would also have to account for the very different ratings pressures and management styles at, say, TVOntario's *The View from Here* and CTV's *W5*. Taking only production methods into account, Canadian documentary programs are clearly distinguishable from each other, and frequently indistinguishable from other program types.

Still others have defined documentary programs according to the intentions of their producers. Magnus Isaacson offers a political as opposed to an aesthetic definition of the genre, arguing that there is "absolutely no way of distinguishing a documentary from even a television news report by using criteria such as narration, pace of editing, [or] film versus video." Real documentaries, he concludes, are those that "offer a vision, a message and are willing to take a stand."[55] The Canadian Independent Film Caucus similarly defines genuine documentary programs as "creative works of an individual ... with sole control over production at every stage."[56] Yet the boundaries of documentary still remain unclear, with Isaacson's definition potentially including and the Film Caucus's excluding virtually every self-styled documentary program ever made in Canada.

Academics can take heart in a similar lack of precision in production and policy discourses. Definitions of documentary have been elaborated, and sometimes enforced, by Canada's courts (for example, in the 1983 libel settlement against the producers of the CBC's *Tar Sands* docudrama),[57] by its political institutions (for instance, the Canadian Senate in hearings concerning the CBC's *The Valour and the Horror* documentary),[58] and by broadcasters themselves (in journalistic policy books, for instance, that define appropriate and inappropriate documentary practices).[59] Similarly, policy regulators have developed their own documentary guidelines to help along the funding process; the Canadian Television Fund essentially distinguishes documentaries from other factual programs on the basis of their length – more than half an hour, according to current rules.[60]

There is certainly no shortage of documentary definitions in Canada, but most of them differ, and all have been subject to revision and reinterpretation. Clearly, policy manuals provide no fixed guides. Meanwhile, as we shall see in chapters 3, 4, and 5, producer definitions themselves have varied widely between departments, between networks, and between networks and independent production companies. Minidocs, docudramas, vérité programs, and current affairs magazines have all been considered documentaries in their time.

How then are *we* to decide the nature of a documentary program? What sort of texts should we include in a documentary study, and what should we leave out? The most prudent strategy might be to abandon altogether the quest for a core canon and a fixed definition of the form. After all, any categorical statement would necessarily involve a selective interpretation of rules and canons of taste that would always (rightly) be open to dispute. Instead, following Steve Neale, we should regard genre definitions as functional and flexible sets of rules used to organize production rather than as innate categories inhabiting a stable corpus of texts.[61] In other words, definitions matter not because they reveal an inner essence of documentary texts but because they are actually used to organize the production, sale, and circulation of programs called "documentaries."

An example may make this point more clear. In 1998 the u.s. Customs Service began defining self-styled documentary programs as either "information projects," which were allowed to shoot in the u.s., or as "commercial entertainment projects," which were not. Under the new guidelines all CBC staff productions were classified as "documentary information" regardless of their program material, while all specialty channel productions were regarded as "commercial entertainment" no matter "how journalistic the tone or educational the content," as journalist Doug Saunders put it at the time.[62] Like most working definitions, the (subsequently revised) customs categories were valuable not because they helped identify "real documentaries" but because they had a material impact on the way programs called documentaries were produced and distributed.

Many other examples can be found of how genre definitions function this way – take the network "naming game" surrounding documentary programs in Canada for the last half century. In 1954 CBC producers briefly considered selling their "documentaries" as "telementaries" or plain old "factual television," to avoid the educational stigma associated with the former term.[63] In 1977 the producers of the CBC's *For the Record* renamed their "docudramas" "topical dramas" largely to avoid the legal responsibilities of documentary programmers. And in 1998 the Global Television network attempted to have many of its "factual programs" recognized as "documentaries" in a bid to gain government funding and support for its dismal Canadian content record. All of these redefinitions had less to do with the changing nature of the programs themselves than with the changing purposes of their producers and handlers. It is those purposes – the "functions" of documentary definitions – that I am chiefly concerned with here.

Thus, I adopt a broad definition of documentary programming, based on producers' and policy-makers' own changing definitions over time. This is not to say that anything goes. There is a certain fixity as well as fluidity to documentary categories, as it is in the interest of those involved to make production practices and viewer expectations more or less predictable and controllable. Clear and relatively stable rules regarding documentary evidence, narratives, and images help producers produce documentary programs, help audiences make sense of them, and help programmers shape the practices of each. To classify *Traders* or *Jerry Springer* as documentary programs would arguably be counterproductive for all.

Such a view has several methodological implications. First, if we embrace a functional rather than fixed definition of documentary programming, we must at the same time avoid an essentialist or implicitly teleological approach to Canadian television history, predicated in the case of documentary on the "search for a Canadian voice"[64] or the "struggle for more and better journalism on Canadian television."[65] Such histories almost invariably culminate in a golden age with attendant ideal program types. This book quite deliberately eschews such an approach, focusing not on an idealized documentary corpus but on a broad range of documentary programs as defined by Canadian producers themselves. Hosted public-affairs shows, journalistic minidocs, women's current-affairs magazines, nature shows, docudramas, vérité investigations, and factual reconstructions (amongst others) are in my view not historical "aberrations" but integral examples of the form, if only because they were so regarded by producers and handlers in their time.[66]

Second, consistent with a functional definition of documentary programming, we should pay particular attention to documentary *contexts* as opposed to just documentary *texts* (or viewers) – that is, to the various production, regulatory, and market sites where particular programs have been shaped, handled, and classified as documentaries. In other words, rather than seeking to determine the "documentariness," "Canadianness," or "progressiveness" of individual programs through textual or the now more fashionable audience analysis, we should undertake a more broadly environmental study of the policies, technologies, media economies, and political terrain within which documentary programs – and audiences – are produced.[67] This study aims to be both textual and contextual in this sense, drawing on interviews, program documents, contemporary reviews, policy statements, and industry data to consider the various institutional contexts within which particular Canadian programs have been defined and distributed as documentaries since 1952.

This contextual approach has further implications for the way we classify and investigate documentary programs. In text-based documentary studies, docudrama programs are frequently regarded as epiphenomena of a larger text – "Canada," for example, and its supposed deep-seated preoccupation with the problematic nature of representation. In a contextual study, however, the proliferation of texts of this type in Canada is seen to have had as much to do with particular technical, organizational, and political circumstances as with any Canadian "zeitgeist." Here, then, programs are seen to reflect not a fixed or essential characteristic of Canadian culture but rather a contingent configuration of social, cultural, and technological forces – specifically, the cash flows, recording technologies, and cultural discourses available to producers at the time the programs were made.

A word about what this history does not include (and might appear to neglect). It does not examine documentaries primarily designed for film distribution and only latterly or incidentally shown on Canadian television. As a result, my choice of programs may seem somewhat peculiar. I have left out many National Film Board productions that received relatively prompt television screenings, such as Tanya Ballantyne's 1967 *The Things I Cannot Change*. On the other hand, I have included Allan King's *Warrendale*, which was not shown on television until thirty years after it was produced. However, it was originally commissioned by the CBC and illustrates, in my view, many of the doubts regarding the ability of public service television to record and interpret Canadian life in the 1960s.

Particularly in the chapters concerning national public service broadcasting, I have focused on CBC productions, to a lesser extent on those of provincial public television networks, and to a lesser extent still on those of Canada's private broadcasters. This is not to accept entirely the Canadian Independent Film Caucus's verdict that the private broadcasters' documentary output is "hardly worth considering."[68] But it does recognize that before the age of the specialty channel, public broadcasters took their documentary and current affairs responsibilities far more seriously than their private counterparts. There are exceptions to this rule, CTV's W5 and a number of documentary specials carried on the private networks being cases in point. But overall, in terms of audience size, program budgets, numbers of programs produced, and critical recognition garnered, public broadcast documentaries have been far more significant than their private counterparts and thus receive much more attention in the earlier parts of this book.

Perhaps most controversially, this book overlooks a good many Quebecois and French language documentaries over the years. This oversight, like the others, is deliberate. This is partly because I believe francophone television to be a separate and distinct cultural apparatus, deserving its own study on almost any given topic. But also, I think documentary television has lacked a degree of cultural significance in Quebec, which in contrast to English Canada has not generally felt the need to distinguish its culture and television programs by their "documentary value." By most accounts, fictional television and not documentary television remains the locus for Quebec's collective identity.[69]

In short, this study focuses mostly on public broadcasting English language documentaries in the early years of Canadian television, and public, private, network, independent, and specialty channel documentaries in the global age. The rest of the book is structured as follows:

Chapter 2 examines the Canadian "broadcast documentary tradition" that developed in the 1930s and '40s and served as a prototype for documentary television in its early years. The history of Canadian documentary film, particularly Grierson's development of an institutional apparatus to "reveal the soul of the nation," as Seth Feldman once put it,[70] is by now familiar, both in its traditional and revisionist guises.[71] Less well known is the more popular and equally dynamic type of documentary programming that was offered on Canadian radio in the first half of the twentieth century. This chapter examines this tradition and the unique forms of production, distribution, and textual organization to which it gave rise.

Chapter 3 considers the early development of Canadian documentary television and, more specifically, the debates concerning representation and meaning that surrounded magazine programs in the 1950s. By drawing attention to these early controversies within Canadian television's "defining" genre in its "golden age," this chapter calls into question a caricature all too common in both Marxist and postmodernist analyses, of public service broadcasting as a quintessential "modern" mass medium dedicated to the production of orderly meanings and contained pleasures. Chapter 4 pursues this theme by examining documentary television in the 1960s, '70s, and '80s and the difficulties it encountered representing the various times and spaces of the nation to itself.

Chapter 5 is concerned with the globalization of documentary television and consists of a general overview of new transnational financing and distribution patterns, along with an analysis of the status of places, public discussions, and meanings in the genre as a result of these changes. Chapter 6 considers what all of the above might tell us about documentary programming, public service broadcasting, and global television in the future.

Each of these chapters is accompanied by analyses of select documentary texts. Chapter 2 focuses on radio documentaries during World War II; chapter 3 on public affairs and women's current-affairs magazines in the 1950s; chapter 4 on vérité programs, historical essays, docudramas, and journalistic reports in the 1960s, '70s, and '80s; and chapter 5 on independent globally oriented productions in the post-national era. By proceeding in this fashion, I hope to shed some light on three main subjects: specific forms of documentary programming, public service broadcasting, and the increasingly global environments in which each has operated in Canadian television's first half century.

2 The Broadcast Documentary Tradition in Canada

In 1961 a CBC public affairs producer offered a "frank" assessment of Canada's documentary films. Most NFB productions were "quite good," noted Bernard Trotter, but too often marred by a tendency towards "drabness, a lack of visual appeal and a preoccupation with abstract do-good subjects." Such problems he saw as most evident in films involving complex information or ideas. In just one short decade, television had "progressed very much further"[1] in the effective presentation of this kind of information than had the NFB, Trotter claimed.

Trotter was speaking in the name of broadcast documentary tradition, and it is that tradition, particularly its origins in Canadian public service radio, that this chapter examines. In the 1930s and '40s, CBC Radio developed a full-fledged documentary apparatus based on aesthetic principles, organizational protocols, and channels of distribution entirely different from those that prevailed in documentary filmmaking and, in the view of broadcasters, entirely more adequate to the task of representing the nation and its public and private affairs. To give a sense of the novelty and significance of Canadian broadcast documentaries in this period, I begin by comparing these with Canadian documentary films. A more detailed study of "progress" in the broadcast field follows.

THE DOCUMENTARY FILM TRADITION IN CANADA

Canadian cinema was conceived as a documentary medium. Federal and provincial governments made early efforts to promote filmmaking about everyday Canadian life, to encourage cultural consciousness at home and political and economic awareness abroad. In the early 1900s filmmakers received grants from Canada's Department of Trade and Commerce and other government agencies to produce portraits of Canada that promoted tourism and immigration from Europe.[2] Government support for filmmaking of the informational-documentary kind became institutionalized with the founding of the Canadian Government Motion Picture Bureau (CGMPB) in 1918 and the National Film Board (NFB) in 1939.

Little effort was made at this time to develop a "film for entertainment" industry in Canada. The National Film Act envisaged a largely functional information medium that would "help Canadians in all parts of Canada to understand ways of living and problems in other parts."[3] Many officials seemed to share the view of NFB director John Grierson that fiction films were somehow at odds with these aims and Canada's national interest. Many saw such films as mindless distractions that threatened to erode Canadians' aesthetic and civic sensibilities – and the country couldn't afford to produce them anyway.[4] Thus most Canadian policy-makers regarded film as a medium that would document the nation and its interests abroad for the benefit of the public.

Cultural officials further envisaged a documentary service that would produce and distribute films quite differently from the rest of the world. Grierson believed documentary film production should be centred around the filmmakers and their interpretive sensibilities rather than the commercial interests of a Hollywood-type studio. Films themselves should be weighted towards the "creative treatment of actuality" rather than the "facile fictions" and "jumpy little postcards with no depth" being turned out by American feature and newsreel companies.[5] Further, documentary distribution should be entirely democratic, exhibiting films in theatrical and non-theatrical venues with the cooperation of community groups across the country.[6] Produced and distributed in these ways, documentary film would offer a unique form of mass communication that by virtue of its sheer relevance and proximity to everyday life would come to "command the imagination" of the nation.[7]

At least, that's how Grierson's project worked in theory. Even sympathetic critics later acknowledged that the National Film Board never quite lived up to its promise. It is doubtful that its films ever "captured the imagination" of Canadians, Grierson's claims apparently based on potential versus actual audiences.[8] Nor were the films much more independent or critically engaged than their Hollywood counterparts, relying as they did on official sponsors,[9] maintaining distant and often authoritarian relations with their citizen-subjects,[10] and generally focusing on individual "victims" rather than the institutional structures that "victimized" them (thereby "running away from social meaning," in the view of Brian Winston).[11] Nor did the films give birth to an alternative film aesthetic, adhering as they mostly did to classic realist traditions of filming, editing, and narrative established in Hollywood features.[12]

But successful or not, the Canadian documentary film project had become a matter of national policy (if not popular interest) by the end of the Second World War. At its height in 1945–46 it was producing over three hundred films a year about Canadian life for distribution across the country and around the world.[13] By the time of the coming of the age of television, then, Canada had developed a massive filmic apparatus with its own modes of production and distribution designed, as critic Seth Feldman later put it, to "reveal the soul of the nation."[14]

DOCUMENTARY AND CANADIAN RADIO

Broadcast documentary was a very different enterprise, with separate roots in the medium of radio and non-filmic reportage. Documentary had become a more or less recognized broadcast genre in the mid-1920s, when "dramatised information programs" concerning history and current events were first aired by private stations in the Maritimes.[15] "Documentary features" quickly became a staple of the the public service broadcasting schedule, when the Canadian Radio Broadcasting Commission, the predecessor of the CBC, listed them as a program type that would be "increased in years to come."[16] By the mid-1930s broadcasters had already come to view documentary programming as a uniquely *educational, entertaining*, and *efficient* way of telling stories about the nation, the benefits of which were seen to result from distinctly non-cinematic modes of production.

Efficiency, for instance, was seen to depend on an assembly-line model of production very much at odds with the small scale, auteur-type system that would come to dominate work at the NFB.[17] Only by means of a "documentary factory," according to some program supervisors, could the corporation produce the enormous and steady volume of material required by its public service mandate. Broadcast crews tended to be much larger and more routine bound than their cinema counterparts. In the late 1930s, for instance, the CBC's *Quarterly Review* used four permanent sound operators, each responsible for separate segments and effects – a fixed division of labour quite unheard of in documentary film production at the time.[18] And while producers tended to be less specialized, often taking part in writing, announcing, and special effects, due to staff shortages, production for most CBC employees was a fairly standardized and predictable affair.

Efficiency was further sought within the confines of the documentary series, rather than the stand-alone documentary production. Individual reports were certainly quite common at the CBC in the 1930s and '40s, particularly in the features department, but they began to be replaced by regular returning shows, including wartime miniseries such as *Fighting Navy* and longer-running domestic programs such as *Les Actualités Canadiennes*. In the late 1940s magazine programs were added to the schedule, offering a diverse collection of actuality items, generally no more than twelve minutes long.[19]

Series production offered a number of advantages to broadcasters. First and foremost it was seen to allow faster and more comprehensive coverage of Canadian events. At *Saturday Magazine*, for instance, producers generally worked on at least three stories at once and often shopped them around to other shows to boost program output.[20] Moreover, the more or less stable production teams of the series were seen to contribute to a documentary craft tradition at the CBC, with programs such as *Open House* and *In Search of Ourselves* serving as training grounds for public affairs producers who went on to work in other information and entertainment programs. Broadcasters also hoped the documentary series would routinize the reception process, by reorganizing home audiences into taste communities loyal to returning shows rather than individual stories. As radio supervisor Harry Boyle later noted, documentary listeners should be encouraged to "keep on coming back" to the CBC.[21] In all these ways, series production was seen to be the cornerstone of effective and reliable information reporting at the CBC.

Broadcasters further developed new technologies to match these efficient new production forms. Radio recording equipment was specifically designed to cover "events where they happened and when they happened" in a way film cameras never could.[22] The CBC made extensive efforts to reduce the weight of its sound recorders in preparation for the Royal Tour of 1939, developing much more portable equipment than the cumbersome camera units used by the NFB in its early (and even later) years. Though the days of the lightweight tape recorder had not yet arrived, some broadcast recording kits weighed only ten pounds and by the mid-1940s could fit into a knapsack.[23] To be sure, such equipment remained scarce and unreliable until the end of the decade, but the corporation quickly introduced regular courses to ensure its wider use.

Technologies were in turn complemented by new programming standards designed to make documentaries more cost-effective and credible. Particularly in the 1940s a more institutionalized and predictable style was imposed on corporate documentaries, with the CBC rejecting what it saw to be the partisan and producer-oriented production traditions of the National Film Board. While there was always some room in its schedule for "personalized portraits, largely the vision of a single producer,"[24] eclecticism was generally frowned upon in documentary broadcasting. Standardized fairness and balance regulations were enacted, amended, and enforced throughout the decade, requiring programs dealing with "controversial issues" to cover a range of "significant views" while "not themselves expressing an opinion."[25] In the public affairs area, a journalistic documentary tradition developed according to which programs were expected to "report on events and not offer interpretations or opinions" – seen to be the province of guest speakers on the CBC's talks programs.[26] From a corporate point of view, standardized journalistic series dealt with current issues with a minimum of risk and a maximum of benefit, regularly and reliably turning out diverse but inoffensive material for the widest "public" imaginable. The corporation thus consciously strove to produce documentary programs for a general audience, which in the public affairs area entailed presenting "comprehensive reportage" in a "comprehensible way."[27]

Producers were keenly aware of the costs involved with these corporate documentary procedures. Point-of-view programs, particularly those outside what the corporation deemed to be a legitimate range of opinion, certainly suffered. So did programs radically experimenting with documentary form; producer Frank Willis's quickly curtailed innovations with sound effects in conjunction with live action was just one early example. But most programmers believed that standardized shows offered more versatility and stylistic range than the drab institutional fare being turned out by the National Film Board in the 1940s.[28] And what the shows lost in diversity, many argued, they made up for in terms of reliability – a reliability dependent not on the style of individual producers but on the well-established technologies and institutional protocols of a documentary *network*.

In short, by the late 1940s broadcasters had developed a new organizational machine for the reporting and interpretation of national affairs. And, as with any machine, the objective was not just uniformity but volume of production. The new technologies and new methods gave rise to levels of documentary output undreamed of in the film world. By 1945–46 six departments of the CBC were producing over eighty documentary programs a year for the English network alone.[29] By 1948 the corporation boasted it could produce a documentary report about an area as distant from Central Canada as Yellowknife with a quick "5000 mile flight and a week's work."[30] Drawing on formidable technical and organizational resources, the corporation could further provide documentary updates and continuing reports. Travelogue producers, for instance, filed weekly updates on their trips across Canada so that listeners could "share the fun of a gypsy life."[31] The Talks and Public Affairs department similarly introduced programs such as *Cross Section,* which promised to provide "accurate, up to the minute and continuing reports on various public affairs subjects."[32] Documentary producers thus promised to explore the full range of Canadian space in more or less serial time – a unique achievement in the postwar documentary world. Radio's new documentary practices were seen to make possible a more or less *complete, immediate,* and *unmediated* portrait of Canada – "unlike anything Canadians had ever heard," as one producer later put it, and superior to anything they had ever seen.[33]

DOCUMENTARY PROGRAMS

The *texts* produced by this organizational machine were also quite unlike anything seen in the film world. Documentary radio, in the view of its producers, was clearly superior to any other information form in terms of its actuality, entertainment value, and democratic potential. To a large extent, *actuality* was equated with location sound, which was regarded as more compelling documentary evidence than any commentary from the studio. Sound from the field became an ever more prominent feature of broadcast programs in the 1940s, particularly wartime broadcasts, with producers such as Matthew Halton and Marcel Ouimet developing a signature style that essentially involved letting the sound tell the story – and "having the wit to be silent."[34] Halton and Ouimet in particular became known as "sound addicts," recording "barrages great and small, the talk of tankmen over their radios, and the sounds of battles overheard."[35] But many of their colleagues in Europe and back in Canada made heroic efforts to get out of the studio and into the open air, their objective being to "faithfully paint the Canadian scene in sound."[36]

In one 1942 report on the opening of the Alaska Highway, producers buried cables under mounds of snow and built bonfires around their recorders to prevent the oiled parts from seizing up.[37] At the front, the corporation developed lighter wired recorders and the first wireless springboard machines cranked by hand to make recordings of up to three minutes in the field.[38] The sounds of war were more often obtained from mobile vans by means of a needle and disk, a method that could be just as unreliable as visual recording technologies at the time. The disks were too hard to cut in winter, too hot to handle in summer and too prone to skips near the action. But with three turntables in some of the vans, radio documentarists could go on recording for as long as they wanted. Just as importantly, they could use the van's playback equipment to produce an edited program ready to be fed into a short-wave transmitter. CBC producers claimed that "no part of the battleground was inaccessible" to their microphones.[39]

Back at home, radio producers sought out the sounds of everyday life, largely unrecorded by other documentarists and information producers of the day. The 1951 documentary *Small Town,* for instance, featured "people working and playing in their accustomed manner." It began in the early morning with three generations of a family "quietly talking as they began their chores," and concluded with the highlight of the show, a group of schoolboys "discussing hunting and fishing at 'the Pond.'"[40] Such ordinary banter had been glaringly absent from Canada's documentary record.

Yet many of the programs were anything but "actual" in a strict sense. Home events were often carefully rehearsed, and spontaneous interaction was the exception, not the rule, in domestic documentaries.[41] Similarly, much of the actuality sound in war programs was more iconic than indexial, depending heavily on archived material. Producers missed many events such as the biggest London air raids, because they already "had" the sounds on tape.[42] But both domestic documentaries and wartime reports made use of actuality material to a degree unknown in the world of information reporting at the time. NFB films, for instance, contained virtually no unrehearsed location sound in the 1940s, because it was hard to capture with 35 mm cameras and even harder to dub into foreign languages (actuality being at odds with the Film Board's production and distribution practices at the time). Similarly, news programs and radio talk shows offered few location sounds other than occasional snatches of rehearsed and mostly official speech.[43] South of the border, American radio contained even less actuality material; war reporters such as Edward R. Murrow offered live dispatches along with some studio dramatizations, but very few sounds from the front lines.[44] In short, the realism of Canadian documentary radio was probably unmatched in its day, with many producers gathering location material shunned or overlooked by Canadian colleagues and American competitors.

Beyond delivering actuality, documentary programming was designed to give listeners *entertainment*. "If it is to be good radio," noted the script editor of *Cross Section,* "documentary must not only inform the listener, but also involve him in the action so that he shares the experiences being presented."[45] During and after the war, producers thus endeavoured to produce documentary "facts" in the most effective radio form possible, and this generally involved not just obtaining location sounds but enhancing them with other types of material. Radio documentary evolved as an art as well as a science, the "art," according to producer Harry Boyle, lying in the effective matching of actuality and non-actuality material such as music and "evocative backgrounds."[46] Even in the heat of battle, for instance, documentary production vans were used not just as recording vehicles but as mobile studios in which location sounds, commentaries, interviews, and sometimes music were dubbed from disc to disc and blended into what one later producer called "more richly constructed sound documentaries."[47]

Back in Canada, producers made further efforts to enhance actuality with the use of sound effects. The CBC established an effects department in Toronto in 1938 and developed special equipment for playback and mixing in the next decade. Creating a documentary "atmosphere" became an increasingly elaborate and ambitious undertaking. One CBC account of a 1954 *Wednesday Night* program about Prohibition has producer Frank Willis castigating his effects crew for recording a gasoline engine rather than the diesel type generally used by Canadian bootleggers at the time, and for slipping in sounds of period locomotives not used in the Atlantic provinces when the story took place.[48] Canadian audiences themselves were, according to legend, able to spot the difference between the sounds of a Hudson and a Wellington aircraft engine, requiring crews for one show to be sent to naval and airbuses across the country to "put to disc new kinds of booms, roars, and rattles heard under varying conditions."[49]

Effects provided not just ambiance but a basic narrative structure, guiding listeners through stories in lieu of more formal filmic-type commentaries. Some producers, for example, used standard boom microphones for main story lines, and specialized cardioid mikes for flashbacks, rarely announcing the time shifts to audiences.[50] By the mid-1940s, documentary effects had emerged as a full-fledged discourse of actuality with its own minutely categorized sounds, standardized production practices, and rigid audience expectations.[51]

Broadcasters worked to further involve audiences by combining documentary and drama in their programs. Of course the mix of fact and fiction was nothing new in Canada; dramatized information had long been a staple in Canadian motion pictures – particularly in newsreels, which had combined actuality footage with faked pictures as a matter of course.[52] More recently, the NFB had included a wide array of (mostly unlabelled) dramatizations in its information films, inspired by Grierson's free mix of fact and fiction in his documentary work. Broadcasters had included dramatized information in their earliest educational and entertainment shows, the first self-styled documentaries in the 1920s and '30s consisting entirely of reenactments and what were called "dramatico-musical" information programs.[53] Pre-war information dramas included strictly instructional fare such as the 1936 *Founding of Empire Day in Canada*; lighter features such as Toronto station CFRB's long-running *Forgotten Footsteps* used interviews, recreations, and music to document exhibits at the Royal Ontario Museum.[54] Wartime docudramas included front-line series such as *Theatre of Freedom* and dramatized farm broadcasts like *Le Reveil Rural* and *The Craigs*. The latter was one of the longest-running series on the English service and the inspiration for a number of similar shows based in other parts of the country. Postwar programs drew upon an even wider array of actuality material, theatre, poetry, and speech to create documentary meanings. A 1951 program on the Mokatum Indians made use of interviews with anthropologists and officials from the Department of Indian and Northern Affairs, limited actuality reporting from a British Columbia reservation, and a "major treatise in free verse" to acquaint listeners with these "first residents of our country."[55]

Dramatization was certainly never considered frivolous or a compromise of pure documentary traditions. Docudramas were highly valued as *information*, dealing with social types and broader national averages unavailable to purely factual observation. In this regard they served as the cornerstone of what the CBC called "sociological journalism," exploring the "tensions, conflict and whole fabric of modern urban life."[56] They were also highly regarded as *fiction*, telling challenging but engrossing stories which it was hoped would fully develop the civic and aesthetic competencies of average Canadians. For Mavis Gallant, writing as a media critic in the late 1940s, it was neither factual programming nor its fiction counterpart that epitomized "culture on the air," but rather a hybrid of the two.[57]

But more than any of these stylistic exercises, radio's most important contribution to the documentary form – and its most effective means of involving audiences in documentary material – was seen to be its *personalized modes of address*. The personalized hosted program was truly a broadcasting innovation. Program hosts had been a staple of North American radio since its earliest years, though in Canada they became much more prominent in the more competitive postwar broadcast market.[58] Stations used hosts and personalities in all types of programming, from music to panel discussions, so as to lend a special tone to distinct segments of the day and shows covering a diverse range of material.[59] Hosts were particularly important in the new magazine programs, ensuring, it was hoped, a steady movement of audiences through an eclectic line-up, from item to item and from week to week.

To do the job, documentary reporters and announcers had to play roles that were entirely new to information radio. Announcers had previously been unable to leave the studio because of techno-logical constraints and union regulations.[60] In the 1940s both announcers and reporters were moved, as audibly as possible, out of the studio and into the field. Wartime documentary journalists were expected to report from the battlefield and to situate them-selves in the actions they were reporting, serving as *delegates* of experience through whom listeners could gain a sense of actuality. At home, travelogue hosts similarly, if less spectacularly, often journeyed across the country to provide their listeners with a "worm's eye view." In these respects, documentaries introduced the "personality" to information radio.

Besides being made more "visible," documentary reporters were expected to speak in new, more personalized ways. Matthew Halton deliberately included ad libs and interruptions in his docu-mentary commentaries, situating himself in the field of action as a full-fledged documentary presence. "Halton spent years searching for just the right tone," noted one contemporary,[61] and a transcript of a 4 July 1944 broadcast from Normandy gives some idea of the new position he assumed in the broadcast documentary text. Unable to provide visual evidence of the new European front, he continually and emphatically *authenticated* the events he was osten-sibly "announcing," "Fortunately for you," he told his listeners, "the sounds as recorded on disc are quiet and tame compared to what they are when we hear them ... Listen to this and imagine it ten times as large."[62]

Halton frequently acted as a moral witness for events that could not be understood in conventional terms. "I hate to tell atrocity stories," he told his listeners in a 30 September 1944 report from the Bredonk Gestapo prison in Belgium, "because I've been telling them so long. Much the same I tell now I told ten years ago about concentration camps in Germany. But there are still people who ask me if the cruelties in the camp can as bad as they say. I think the camp should be described ... There is in this place an evil memory. You wonder for a moment if there is any hope for a world which could produce such a monstrosity."[63]

All of this was unprecedented, not just because of the length at which Halton held forth but because of the intimacy of his tone and the varied positions from which he addressed his audience. He spoke not just for the corporation, but for the public and its sense of wonder and outrage, and for himself as a thinking and feeling person – in a voice that was anything but institutional. Again the contrast with other forms of information media at the time was remarkable. Unlike his filmic counterparts who were encouraged to read their scripts in as detached a way as possible, Halton appeared as the author as well as the animator of documentary discourse. And unlike his newscaster colleagues, he was entirely unbound by network rules requiring scripted and anonymous speech devoid of any "colouring" or "inflection."[64] His adoption of a more direct and personal tone, coupled with his role as a delegate to the action, was of course not just a personal project. It was in fact a deliberate effort by the network to align its corporate texts more closely with the "personal space" of the Canadian home, "linking the war effort," as one CBC annual report put it, "to the life of the individual."[65] Strictly speaking, Halton and his employers attempted to make his reports *come to life*, the corporation citing with approval a contemporary cartoon of a Canadian family diving under the furniture at the sound of his voice.[66]

In various ways and for a number of reasons, then, broadcasters worked to make their programs more eclectic, more immediate and more involving than the rather sterile institutional discourses of documentary film and information broadcasting. Their objective, it seems, was nothing less than to make documentary popular for the first time in its history. The corporation clearly had high hopes for the genre, documentary programming being "one of its most pop-ular types," the CBC claimed in its 1943–44 annual report; its audiences compared favourably with those for newscasts and even commercial entertainment programming.[67] Producers further insisted (plausibly though without much hard evidence) that docu-mentary radio programs were "far more popular" than documen-tary films in Canada.[68]

Finally, beyond popularizing the form as such, broadcasters worked to make documentary more democratic. Producers sought out new speakers largely absent from other forms of actuality reporting in Canada. In 1938, for instance, the corporation's Special Broadcasting unit departed from its own official speeches and events format and introduced *Street Scenes*, a series based on "man-in-the street interviews from various points across the Dominion."[69] Similarly, the Talks and Public Affairs department promised "simple factual recounting[s] of the experiences and understandings of the man-in-the-street."[70] By 1940 the corporation was able to claim that an "admixture of expert and layman testimony" had "leavened [its programs] to appeal to almost all tastes."[71] It continued these efforts after the war with programs such as *Log Drive 1953,* which followed its subjects "by tugboat, freight car, truck or pony" to "talk with them in their bunkhouses or houseboats where they live."[72] Others such as the 1953 special *Jarvis Street* aimed to "get away from the traditional documentary and let communities tell their own stories from the inside."[73] Broadcast documentarists thus made some efforts to let Canadians speak for themselves in the age of mass communication.

Of course, these programs were hardly simple or transparent records of community life. Radio's relations with its documentary subjects were generally complicated and problematic, and as a democratic project broadcast documentary was always subject to structural limitations. While producers boasted of their proximity to average Canadians, their own accounts often tell a different story. "We expected to find a primitive place," noted the producers of *Yellowknife Report*, part of the CBC's 1948 *Armed Forces in Peacetime* series, "but instead we were billeted in a large stucco hotel built at a cost of $200,000 with an up-to-date cocktail bar and lounge and all the trimmings."[74] Under such conditions, producers admitted, the search for "local characters" was often pointless and unproductive. In fact many expeditions into Canada's hinterland seemed more like journalist junkets than honest ethnographic exercises.

Areas outside Toronto and Canada's major cities tended to be exoticized, and featured as "Other" zones in documentary reports. One producer said he felt like an "earth man landing on another planet" when preparing a 1954 report on Cornwallis Island for the program *Canadian Scene*: "The different colours and bleak terrain were something quite outside my experience."[75] Moreover, the people of Canada's margins tended to be positioned firmly within an ideological (Euro-) reading of identity in the programs, with difference constantly being defined (and sometimes denied) in relation to metropolitan culture. Early programs positioned native Indians as largely generic subjects of a postwar national project, who "like ourselves," noted one program description, "have a contribution to make to Canadian life."[76] The main character of the 1951 docudrama *Mokatum* emerged as a hero only after waging a successful war of "common sense against the superstition in which she was raised."[77] Even the most liberal-democratic programs of the 1940s and '50s, then, were almost entirely concerned with an administrative problematic of how to assimilate marginal communities to the "white man's world."[78] Early programs on immigrant communities similarly regarded difference as a curiosity to be geographically and discursively contained. Many shows took on the form of a colonial jaunt, a 1951 feature report on Vancouver's "oriental section," for instance, engaging Harvey Lowe ("perhaps the only Chinese disc jockey in North America") to assist host Eileen Laurie on her "walks into Chinatown."[79]

Women were also carefully positioned in radio's documentary record and sometimes excluded from it. True, documentaries dealing with gender issues had been a regular part of the public service schedule since 1939, and though the shows were often elitist in tone (featuring women with "specialized knowledge or experience to share"),[80] many attempted to critically address the role of women in public life. The 1948 series *Women in Business* focused on the "equality of the sexes which is theoretical and not practical in nature," while other programs overseen by producer Marjorie McEnaney launched similar "social investigations."[81] On the whole, however, women's issues were defined as domestic matters at the CBC, banished to daytime schedules and shaped within the confines of the less prestigious (though generally more popular) magazine formats, whose short breezy segments were seen to be more suitable for the busy homemaker. Programs were thus scheduled and stylized with women's "natural" domestic roles in mind, and in this way women were subordinated within the CBC documentary lineup, both institutionally and discursively.[82]

It is easy to dismiss these programs as incorporation and surveillance exercises.[83] But the same can be said of other forms of actuality reporting at the time. Broadcast documentary at least had the merit, in the view of its producers, of *attempting* to let its subjects speak – in however flawed and editorially compromised a way. In liberal-democratic terms, the programs were a vast improvement over the "helpless victim" portraits of Griersonian cinema, and the "spoken-for mass" snapshots of other types of information broadcasting. Enlisting new subjects, and encouraging them to speak within less formal types of social reportage, radio documentarists were clearly attempting to construct an alternative to the rigid and exclusionary discourses of Canadian information reporting at the time. "Our goal," claimed producer Harry Boyle, was to "record in their own voices as many Canadians as possible."[84]

In these ways, documentary radio perhaps extended the boundaries of Canadian public life. Broadcast documentarists certainly expended a good deal more energy than their counterparts at the NFB in getting "average" Canadians to speak – not an easy task given their "stiffness and reluctance" in this regard.[85] Documentarists also provided these new subjects with topics for discussion in ways their colleagues did not, seeking out daring new stories just as newscasters were pledging to exclude "all items of a sensational or scandalous nature" from their programs.[86] Documentary series such as *In Search of Ourselves* dealt with "emerging new issues" of human relations in the 1940s with stories like "The Disappointed Couple," "Too Old to Work," and an "Alcoholic Woman." Producer Len Peterson was constantly on the lookout for items deserving public attention, once "trotting downstairs and hunting up" his landlady for a feature story on menopause.[87]

Beyond merely *reflecting* or *restricting* public discussions, then – as a liberal or Marxist model might suggest – documentary programming may have *enabled* new forms of civic life. By training new speaking subjects and broadening their range of discussable topics, the medium created a broader and more inclusive field of discourse across the country.[88] In helping to develop new forms of public life in the age of mass communication, broadcast documentary was perhaps truer to the Griersonian democratic project than was documentary film itself.

In all these respects, by the early 1950s Canadian broadcasters had developed a full-fledged documentary tradition with its own modes of production and its own attendant ideas of public service. And though this tradition could be as predictable and formulaic as critics charged, it produced programs that were arguably more diverse, more involving, and more democratic than any known form of Griersonian cinema or information broadcasting. From a historical perspective, then, the broadcast tradition is best seen not as a pale copy of documentary film or broadcast journalism but as an entirely distinct information form – an *alternative* documentary model for the television age.

CONCLUSION

In 1949 the Massey Commission began its hearings concerning the future of broadcasting and culture in Canada. For the first time the radio and film visions of television and documentary were laid out in full, back to back. The details of the NFB and CBC submissions to the commission are instructive. The NFB clearly viewed Canadian television as an extension of documentary film. Films about Canadian life would "be to television as the disc is to broadcasting."[89] The Film Board stressed that it had been researching a wide range of technical aspects of television and had even assigned a producer to NBC headquarters in New York, "in order to bring back ... experience of the broadest possible range in the field."[90] But clearly its own plans for Canadian television were largely instructional. Programs the NFB had in mind for Canadian prime time included *Youth Hosteling in Canada*, a returning series following a group of cyclists through various regions; *Cruising to Canada*, detailing "how pleasure boats can reach Canada by coastal and inland waters"; and *Winter Carnival*, dealing with "attractions and tourist accommodations in Canada in the off season."[91]

The CBC, on the other hand, viewed television as an essentially popular medium catering to an array of tastes. To be sure, it sometimes took the conventional public service line that information and entertainment should be separate and not entirely equal parts of the TV schedule: "The CBC takes into account that there are many different tastes, needs and wants from broadcasting and that they cannot all be met at the same time," the corporation noted in its submission, "so we try in different program periods to meet different sections of audience tastes."[92] More frequently, however, and more integrally to its programming strategy, the corporation spoke about the need for hybrid shows that would simultaneously inform and entertain the general public: "There are many programs of different types of an informative character. [In radio] special effort has been made with considerable success to develop new techniques for building programs that carry useful information and stimulation to thought, and also attract and hold the interest of large numbers of listeners."[93]

Documentary television in Canada was clearly conceived in light of this more populist broadcast tradition, drawing on production practices and forms proper to both fiction and non-fiction programming. It is the history of this genre in its early stages that I want to examine in the next chapter, a history I believe tells us a good deal about the evolution of the documentary in Canada, but more, about public service television and culture in the modern age.

3 Documentary in the Early Years of Canadian Television

In May 1952, as CBC TV prepared to go to air, producer Mavor Moore explained the program strategy of public service television in Canada.[1] First and foremost, he noted, Canada's new network would do away with the strict separation of information and entertainment fare so common in other countries. "Not to say there cannot be programs designed for formal education or entertainment," he explained, "but merely that the [area between the two] may be more fruitful than presupposed."[2] Canadian television would thus stake out a "middle ground" between British (information oriented) and U.S. (entertainment) television, featuring documentary and public affairs programs that Canadians would actually choose to watch in a more or less competitive North American broadcast market.

It is these "middle ground" information programs that I want to examine in this chapter, specifically, documentary programs as they developed in the first decade and a half of Canadian television. I begin with an examination of the *theory* of documentary television envisaged by critics and policy-makers in the 1940s and '50s, as well as its *practice* in the years that immediately followed. The gap between theory and practice tells us much about the relationship of public service broadcasting to "modern" culture.

DOCUMENTARY TELEVISION IN
THEORY: THE MASSEY COMMISSION
AND CANADIAN EDUCATORS

In the late 1940s and early '50s, policy-makers in Canada viewed television as an essentially pedagogic service with documentary programming as one of its cornerstones. The Massey Commission, which presided over the introduction of Canadian television in 1952, argued that television should inform Canadians about various aspects of their lives. Much more, it should contribute to a general upgrading of critical analytical skills on the part of average Canadians. Documentary programming was seen to be particularly suited to the accomplishment of this task. Documentary television, like its film counterpart, would instill in Canadians a "concern with real as opposed to synthetic situations."[3] The commissioners believed the documentary form would evoke an "awareness of life rather than an escape from it"[4] and encourage a sensitivity to the particularities of place, sadly absent in other forms of mass culture.[5] As both a "place reflecting" and "issue engaging" genre, documentary broadcasting would serve as a countervailing force against American television's homogenous world of fantasy. Radio documentaries, the commissioners noted hopefully, had already been "of great value in making better citizens of us, in that they awaken our critical faculties,"[6] and clearly they had similar expectations for the genre on television. In short, documentary programming would be a key element of Canada's postwar cultural nationalist project.[7]

Policy makers and educators also had high hopes concerning the way the programs would be produced and watched. The Massey Commission, for instance, called for the maintenance of a proper boundary between information and entertainment programs, noting with concern the hiring of public affairs announcers with "no special knowledge other than broadcasting," the cultivation of certain "base forms of popular appeal," and the emergence of subjective modes of address and opportunities for audience involvement.[8] The commission urged the maintenance of "good taste" and recommended that educational experts be consulted at every stage of production.[9]

In a similar spirit policy-makers and educators recommended a sober deployment of images and sounds in the new programs.

According to the Massey Report, television images should be used with restraint and purpose, with programs "teach[ing] not by pictorial or dramatic effects but by coherent and logical presentation of fact."[10] Narratives should similarly adhere to a rigorous cumulative expository structure, along the lines of the National Film Board's long form information films.[11] Documentary programs, it was hoped, would be "in quality and and authority comparable to the scholarly talk ... acceptable to the expert and enjoyed by the layman."[12] Canada's information television aesthetic should thus be governed by well-established (mostly literary) principles of representation.

Finally, the commission and many of its academic interveners recommended close supervision of the ways information programs were *watched*. Policy-makers and educators argued that viewing documentaries at home should ideally be rather like viewing documentaries at the cinema, the audiovisual information venue of the previous decade. Home viewers were to be focused, engaged and, as much as possible, collectively involved with the new documentary shows, concentrating on the programs and then discussing them as a family or perhaps with their neighbours.[13] Children might watch documentary programs after school and be tested on them the next day,[14] though even here, according to Dr Fred Rainsberry, the CBC's assistant director of children's TV broadcasts, the younger public affairs audience should "be discouraged from long periods" of viewing and "should not lie on the floor." Their television time should be monitored with "constant vigilance by men and women with taste and judgment."[15] For both children and adults, information programs and their educational counterparts should be scheduled at precise but varying times, so as to discourage lazy viewing habits associated with American audiences. In time, it was hoped, Canadian viewers would come to appreciate the rigour of the new schedule, just as the idealized "comprehensive" listeners of radio shows like the CBC's *Wednesday Night* had learned to appreciate eclectic information-drama-music fare, effortlessly making the switch from genre to genre, often for hours on end, and "much better for it," according to critic Mavis Gallant.[16]

Canadian television in its founding charter thus dedicated itself to the production of difficult programs for disciplined audiences. In the postwar era, most policy-makers and educators regarded television as a functional apparatus with which representations of Canada could be systematically produced and consensually understood within more or less orderly networks of signification. Documentary television in Canada was conceived, in theory at least, as a *modern project*: one whose meanings and pleasures could be regulated in accordance with the well-established hierarchies of knowledge and representation of Canadian "high culture." In this respect, according to one Canadian educator, CBC TV would be "business as usual."[17]

DOCUMENTARY TELEVISION IN PRACTICE: THE CBC'S MIDDLE GROUND

But what about documentary television in practice? Did the defining genre of Canadian television's "golden age" even loosely adhere to the pedagogic protocols prescribed by the Massey Commission? An analysis of organizational files, promotional documents, contemporary cultural criticism, and the programs themselves suggests a far more complicated picture than that laid out in public service television's founding charter and in subsequent analyses that have taken its injunctions at face value.

First and perhaps most crucially, documentary programs had to be not just pedagogical but *popular* in ratings terms. Documentary television was launched within a highly competitive market, more than four years after the introduction of regular service in the United States – which meant that up to 100,000 Canadian households were already receiving American channels by the time the programs went on the air.[18] Public service documentary programs not only had to attract new viewers but win many more over from their U.S. competition. While CBC officials insisted that the integrity of their programs would never be compromised in this new market and that commercial pressures would never have any direct impact on content,[19] they were clearly concerned about the possible drain away of domestic information audiences even in Canadian television's first year of service. These market conditions led many producers to advocate a "concentration on lighter information programs," according to officials at a 1953 National Program Office meeting.[20]

Producers also recognized that the new world of television made documentary and public affairs audiences virtually impossible to regulate in the ways envisaged by the Massey Commission. Viewers, for instance, would be hard to organize into community circles, and broadcasters would have to learn to address themselves, as one producer put it, to "one person at a time," learning to "compete with bridge, poker, gossip, and many factors not encountered in stage or screen."[21] Even children would have to be consistently entertained in the documentary and public affairs area; as the producers of the information program *Junior Magazine* noted, "whereas the young viewer may have to pay attention to lessons in school, in the living room he has only to switch channels."[22]

These were hardly the pedagogically available viewers forecast in policy documents and educational briefs. As columnist Alan Sangster ruefully noted in *Canadian Forum*, "what they [Canadian audiences] now demand, and all they will accept from TV is straightforward entertainment. As a result of years of exposure to American commercial television, their viewing habits may already be set."[23] Thus even cultural nationalists had largely ceased to regard the new public affairs audience as a sub-species of the *comprehensive viewer,* able to take up serious and popular audience positions as required by the public service text; or even as a *segmented public,* the lower orders of which might eventually be led to better things. Instead, documentary viewers came to be seen as a *general audience* whose needs and desires must be be taken as more or less given – that is, accommodated or at least addressed by the programs themselves. New markets and new modes of reception were thus seen to render documentary television and its pleasures quite unamenable to conventional cultural control.

NEW MODELS FOR DOCUMENTARY PROGRAMMING

Numerous discussions took place in the earliest years of Canadian television concerning how documentary might offer a public service while at the same time holding its own in a more or less competitive broadcast line-up. How could documentary programming adapt itself to this new market environment? And more specifically, how could it stake out a "middle ground," informing while at the same time entertaining viewers? In April 1952 the American producer

Gilbert Seldes was invited to give a ten-day workshop on "fact and fiction" programs based on his book *Writing for Television*, and his prognosis for documentary was optimistic if unconventional. Documentaries, Seldes had noted in his book, were cheaper than variety shows with their "orchestras, ballets and multiple sets" and might even be profitable if their material was "tractable enough to be worked into entertainment."[24] He went on to suggest a number of concrete steps to make the genre popular.

Programs should be as eclectic as possible, he advised. The moment viewers saw an expert or talking head, they would "want something else as well" – namely, video footage – and the onus was on programmers to stress the "videoactive element."[25] The "entire range of the documentary image" should be used, including "maps, diagrams which can be set in motion ... [and] whatever is visible to the human eye, to the telescope or microscope."[26] Narrative diversity should also be a feature of the new programs, and here documentaries could look to quiz shows and variety programs for new ways of telling stories and building suspense.[27] Documentaries should be composed of distinct "billboarded" segments, which would be announced as upcoming segments of the program.[28] Eclectic, fast-paced shows were also crucial. "Under the Big 'D' for Documentary," Seldes summed up, "are other d's – for demonstration, dramatization and discussion."[29] The great virtue of the fact program was that it could "combine many techniques."[30]

Commercially viable documentary shows must be more personal and direct in the way they addressed the audience, in contrast to the distant and sometimes severe expositions of documentary cinema. "You will discover after a few months in the business," noted Seldes, "that 'documentary' seems to deal exclusively with unpleasant subjects, such as Communism, crimes, syphilis and the like."[31] He recommended a lighter line-up and a more personal touch. Stories should deal with everyday life and be both new and "immediately familiar" to the viewer.[32] Hosts should connect stories to the space and time of the home audience, bringing each item "back down to earth" and into the orbit of the immediate present – as represented by the news line-up.[33] In these respects, personalities would be the medium through which documentaries would speak directly to viewers. All in all, by becoming more varied and intimate in a *televisual* sense, documentaries had every chance of being "rating winners."[34]

Even if they found Seldes's unabashedly commercial approach "alarming in certain respects," CBC officials agreed that documentaries must be entirely revamped for television.[35] According to the CBC's supervising producer of Public Affairs, Eugene Hallman, magazine shows would be the showcase of the CBC documentary schedule. Magazines first of all had the advantage of being *different* from documentary films, thereby drawing attention to the CBC and its work in public affairs. While Hallman stressed that he had "no quarrel with the Film Board's approach to documentary," he insisted the CBC should never abandon its own "direct responsibility for doing shows in the documentary field." Unless the corporation developed its own distinct type of documentary programming, a great many subjects would "fall into [the NFB's] hands by default."[36] Documentary magazines would also allow comprehensive public affairs coverage in which fast paced, eclectic line-ups could deal with a "large number of topics in a short amount of time." This would be crucial as the corporation came to deal with "special interests ... none of whom will get the time they would like to have" on television.[37] Finally, magazine programs promised to be *commercially sustainable*. If the success of NBC's *Today* show and CBS's *See It Now* was anything to go by, magazines might even replace some light entertainment shows on the Canadian prime-time schedule.[38] In short, documentary magazines would allow the CBC to fulfil its public service mandate while holding its own in the new information television market.

What Seldes's and Hallman's suggestions shared was an aversion to cinematic and literary modes of representation and an insistence that documentary come into its own as a distinctly televisual form. There seems in fact to have been little debate over these points in Canadian television circles, and the popularized types they advocated quickly dominated the CBC schedule. The corporation did offer conventional longish form documentaries in the mid-1950s on programs such the NFB's *Window on Canada* and its own educational series *Explorations* and *Premier Plan*. But these were the exceptions to the rule. Most documentary programs were in the magazine tradition, featuring diverse departmentalized items under a variety of subject headings in which thematic links were not immediately apparent. *Newsmagazine* focused on stories behind the news, covering everything from "bums to beauties, crime to politics" in its first year on the air.[39] The current affairs series *Close-Up* in its first two seasons showcased items on beat-niks, unwed mothers, mixed marriages, communism, and homo-sexuality. For its part, the educational series *Explorations* offered visual treatments of the "less well known aspects of society and the world of science."[40] These programs were supplemented by a range of departmentalized features. Arts programs such as *Scope* and *Quest* included "drama, music, dance and the documentary" to present a wide range of subject matter.[41] Travelogue series such as *Here and There* and *Country Canada* documented people and scenes across Canada. General interest shows such as *Graphic*, and *Champ libre* on the French network, offered a wide range of social, political, cultural, and human interest stories. Television's documen-tary line-up was thus designed to cover "every conceivable topic under the sun."[42]

But beyond its breadth, documentary television was celebrated for its unique *actuality* value. CBC Television, like CBC Radio, committed itself to a broadcast type of actuality underwritten by network notions of objectivity. Televisual truth was first of all seen to be guaranteed by the sheer size and reach of the CBC organiza-tion – by the bureaucracy of the television network. Systematized production within a national network system, it was hoped, would produce more stories about more people, places, and things in Canada than ever before. Its programs, the CBC claimed, were being produced by some of the largest documentary crews in history. *Graphic* reportedly required a team of one hundred "highly trained people each week," including twenty planners, writers, and researchers in Toronto and twenty camera and sound technicians in remote units, stationed to pick up live stories in Montreal, Toronto, and Ottawa. When stringers from around the country were added to the mix, *Graphic* was seen to be "one of CBC Television's most ambitious projects to date."[43] Even smaller shows took advantage of relatively generous budgets and efficient produc-tion practices to "show more of Canada to Canadians than ever before." *Newsmagazine* used crews of two to five people and took anywhere from an hour to a week to shoot a story.[44]

Broadcast actuality was further seen to be guaranteed by network *rules and regulations*. In 1952 and early 1953, officials at the National Program Office tried to ensure "continuing supervision of regional and network public affairs programs" to maintain "con-sistent standards of accuracy, objectivity and balance."[45] Rules were later introduced to ensure closer supervision of stories by regional and national series producers.[46] Officials insisted that regional and contributing producers needed guidance as they had "little background in CBC policy ... and little time to weigh the implications of program ideas, speakers and methods of presentation."[47] Only in these ways could the programs conform to network standards of documentary objectivity.

Relations with documentary *sources* were also rigidly structured to meet the perceived needs of the public service network. Television documentarists were instructed to research and assemble documentary programs as much as possible "in house" in the 1950s, and to cooperate with academic experts and filmmakers at the NFB on a limited and formal basis. In 1954 the CBC's National Program Office called for closer supervision of Film Board TV productions to "achieve a product that will fit our needs and fit our schedule."[48] The next year Eugene Hallman recommended the severance of official connections with Canadian universities, which had contributed to many radio productions, though he supported limited cooperation with other education and community groups. The CBC's supervising producer of Public Affairs let it be known that programs should henceforth be produced as much as possible with the corporation's own permanent film crews who "understand the purposes, plans and process of the show."[49] In these ways, CBC's documentary producers worked to develop a fully standardized and largely self-sufficient information network in its first years of service.

Finally, documentary truth was seen to be guaranteed by the new recording *technologies* of television. "As a symbol of TV's ability to roam the country we display the TV camera," announced the CBC *Times* in February 1953, complete with an inventory of "lenses and attachments able to do for the TV image roughly what binoculars and a small telescope can do for a spectator's vision."[50] New technologies were seen to make entirely new parts of Canadian available for inspection, from the furthest reaches of the nation to the most intimate zones of the human body. The 1956 feature *Arctic Essay,* for instance, used the new equipment to produce the first sync sound documentary of the Arctic, matching its images with everything from the sounds of barking huskies and hovering helicopters right down to the "sharp tick of echo sounders recording new depths of the ocean."[51] Stop motion photography allowed the 1960 documentary feature *Thread of Life* to show chromosomes dividing – requiring a set of car headlights to allow the cells to be seen through a microscope, and a cooling system to keep the light from destroying the cells.[52]

Some programs like *Close-Up* offered intrusive forms of surveillance, "searching new looks" into unexamined areas of Canadian social experience. Others such as *Explorations* promised more extensive types of representation, "sociological journalism" with which to "explore the whole fabric of urban life."[53] But all modes of documentation were implicitly contrasted with the provincialism and perceptual limitations of direct experience. "Canada like you've never seen it before," promised the magazine program *Graphic*, pointing to its "100 receiver feeds from all along the new transnational microwave network."[54] Documentary technologies promised not just the pleasures of delegation – with programs serving as the "next best thing to being there" – but the pleasures of mastery. This was a new sort of modern meta-experience that was better than being there and more like being everywhere, like never before.

Many public affairs producers believed there was nothing to match the actuality value of documentary television, either on film or in broadcasting. Documentary programs seemed to offer a uniquely comprehensive portrait of Canadian life, more visual and compelling than anything offered by radio, more neutral and all-seeing than anything dreamed of by Canadian documentary film and more capable of making sense of the world than any short newscast or live location feed. True, some early sceptics believed the latter might make recorded documentaries obsolete, but initial experiments in the field were not promising. A 1956 live broadcast recording "a half hour in the life" of the Barrie family of Guelph, Ontario, took a crew of twenty-eight over two days to rig the remote equipment – and after all that, the main subject, Earl Barrie, excused himself early in the broadcast to go the bathroom, never to return.[55] Live broadcasts offered neither the information (nor the entertainment) value of recorded documentary shows. As Mary Ross noted in her review of the first coast-to-coast live broadcast in 1958, the "camera darted about the Dominion in every direction, as innocent of an itinerary as a water bug" for the first hour and a half of the broadcast, which apparently consisted of mostly frozen images and bystanders photographed from the knees down. "So far," Ross concluded, "live broadcasts are of limited value in recording the daily and even second-by-second happenings over

3,000 miles away."[56] With competition such as this, documentary television seemed to offer an altogether more complete picture of Canada than any other audiovisual form of its day.

And a more *engrossing* picture as well: television's greatest contribution to documentary, beyond its actuality value, was seen to be its intimate and involving style.[57] Not only, it was hoped, would viewers believe what they were seeing on screen; they would also take responsible pleasures in the viewing. This was indeed the essence of the documentary "middle ground." Producers plumbed the vaults of television's (admittedly limited) early stylistic repertoire to offer a range of entertaining new sights and sounds. Sidney Newman, in his work for *Graphic*, drew freely on the New York tradition of live location theatrical programming which he had studied at NBC headquarters in the late 1940s as an intern for the National Film Board. Others such as Thom Benson utilized their experiences on the stage to produce a more dramatic kind of documentary approach. Documentary producers also developed more specifically televisual modes of expression. The makers of *Graphic, Close-Up,* and *Champ libre*, amongst others, interspersed their documentary stories with "immediate picture transmissions" made possible by the CBC's expanding microwave facilities. And while most of the live material came from the studio, such a mix was still seen to give the programs a more "immediate impact."[58] Producers also experimented widely with 16 mm film (which the CBC had adopted as a production standard because of the prohibitive costs of its 35 mm counterpart), and so were able to introduce a lighter and more mobile feel to their work.[59] They further made early and extensive use of the new lighter-weight cameras and recorders which appeared in the 1950s, some of them developed at the National Film Board. In the late 1950s television documentarists distanced themselves almost entirely from a film aesthetic by videotaping many of their subjects (a practice largely shunned at the NFB),[60] developing this means of recording into a "fine science and art."[61] In all these respects, documentary producers radically changed the look of documentary in Canada – at least as seen on television.

They also experimented widely with sound and graphics to make their programs more compelling. Documentary music became an aesthetic form in its own right with composers like NFB veteran Louis Applebaum developing an "art of musical bridges" to link together the short scenes and segments of documentary magazines.[62]

Meanwhile, storyboard and layout artists worked to link magazine segments and "create first and final impressions of the show,"[63] with the CBC promoting the work of graphic designer Fred Kruper as an "emerging new art form."[64]

One early example of the new television aesthetic was the program *Tabloid*, whose producer, Ross McLean, had been "exerting himself for years to develop new ways of making information entertaining."[65] McLean had started out at the CBC producing "radio cartoons" (actuality sound vignettes).[66] His motto for the *Tabloid* series was "facts with fun," and he promised that "talks, demonstrations, documentary features, interviews, animated graphics, actuality panel discussions, press conferences and chorus lines [would] continue to be mixed up in the *Tabloid* potpourri."[67]

To be sure, the programs were not always the hotbeds of experimentation promised by their programmers. There were oft-cited charges that television was nothing more than "radio with pictures." Documentaries were hardly the main butt of such criticism, but they could be stodgy, as producers themselves admitted. Qualified personnel were in short supply which obviously curtailed the development of an information television aesthetic. Moreover, the ones who were available had generally started out in radio and sometimes had a hard time imagining the visual sides of stories. Ratings pressures exacerbated the situation, weeding out programs that were "too far out." The experimental arts and documentary series *Scope* was dropped by four CBC affiliates in 1955 and carried by the others "only under protest,"[68] while *Graphic* was rumoured to have been cancelled to appease the Fowler Commission and its demands for more commercially sustainable programming.[69] Experimental programs were also held back by technical-organizational constraints, relying as they did on camera and sound work provided by the CBC film unit and engineering department, both reputedly hostile to innovative work.[70] But on balance, producers such as Felix Lazarus seemed to feel that the new technologies and organizational resources of broadcasting created more opportunities than they prevented.[71] Public Affairs personnel further noted, though not always gratefully, that they were constantly spurred on to do something different by Canada's growing cadre of television critics; columnists such as Marian Smith and Miriam Waddington were early champions of documentary and public affairs producers' attempts to "do something outside [information television's] well worn ruts."[72] And whether the critics were in fact as "avidly read [by producers] in search of critical direction" as they claimed,[73] it seems clear that their support contributed to the development of documentary as an information and entertainment form.

Producers further tried to keep viewers interested by *personalizing* the form, that is, by focusing on people with whom they could identify in more intimate and subjective ways. Early programs worked hard to present more revealing portraits of their subjects and to present them as something more than institutional or demographic stand-ins. *Graphic* promised to visit ordinary Canadians where they lived and worked, if necessary bringing them to the studio, because "people are always interested in what the other fellow is doing."[74] *Newsmagazine*, following the model of Edward R. Murrow's *Person to Person* reports on CBS, offered man-behind-the-job portraits, including a 1956 portrait of Governor-General Vincent Massey "operating a sewing machine and feeding a banana to a monkey."[75]

Producers also encouraged their subjects to speak more directly and revealingly to viewers at home. In 1956, for instance, *Explorations* aired "Speak Your Mind," an "unrehearsed film of students brought before the camera by their principal."[76] *Skid Row*, a 1957 documentary vérité piece produced by Allan King, featured vagrants who would "tell their stories to the camera, openly, often with rigour and with surprising fluency."[77] *Candid Eye*, a regular series produced by Tom Daly of the NFB, sought to "evoke the real character of people" in a variety of situations.[78] Documentary subjects for the new actuality reports were sometimes reluctant: "Speak Your Mind" relied on old-fashioned schoolyard discipline to elicit testimony from its grade school subjects, as a transcript of the opening segment indicates:

PRINCIPAL [AND HOST] HAROLD WHITELY: Boys and girls, I would like to hear your discussion about fears, because I think it would be more interesting to grown-ups than the topic you keep switching to – money. How do you feel about that?
BOY STUDENT: I think you're right, sir. I think we should talk about fears.
PRINCIPAL WHITELY: Not because I say so ...
GIRL STUDENT: Actually sir, most of us don't like to admit our fears ...

Skid Row's street people only appeared in the film when they knew it was "worth a couple of bucks," and the producers and their social worker assistants ran into trouble when they "ran out of small change and had to keep [the main characters] together by force of personality."[79] *Candid Eye* resorted to what it called "multi camera techniques" so that interviewees never knew which camera was filming them.[80] Such interview techniques were not unusual. Producers and their surrogates frequently resorted to bribery, cajolery, and various forms of coercion to elicit "free speech" from the new personages of the documentary program. But the result, they claimed, was more intimate portraits of Canadians across the country, which in turn allowed audiences to relate to programs in new ways. "We must do whatever we can to both step back and get up close, to get our audience thinking *and* involved with the shows," argued *Explorations*'s Jo Kowin.[81] Viewers were thus situated squarely in documentary television's information-entertainment "middle ground."

Producers also worked through the person of the host to make documentaries more informative *and* involving. These personalities had been slow to develop at the CBC where radio public affairs announcers had not been allowed to introduce themselves by name until 1936, and even then only as "part of a carefully controlled and closely watched experiment."[82] Early hosts were recruited from the ranks of authority, which included only "educated men ... possessed of clear Canadian voices with a distinctly masculine quality."[83] These were hardly familiar or personable types; indeed, in its early years, documentary radio seemed determined to preclude any opportunities for audience "identification." By the 1940s, however, hosts had clearly assumed a more prominent position in documentary discourse, allowing new forms of subjective involvement with the shows (see chapter 2).

Television similarly embraced the idea of the documentary and public affairs personality, albeit tentatively. *Newsmagazine* started out in 1952 as "little more than a TV counterpart of a newsreel or film ... impersonal and briefly factual."[84] Early discussions regarding documentary series, however, recognized the importance of a "host of an Ed Murrow type ... giving something of his personal stamp to the program [and] becoming a personality with whom the audience can identify."[85] "We would certainly have trouble allowing such a host to take as independent a line as Murrow does," noted Eugene Hallman, "but in true Canadian fashion we should be able to work something out."[86] Women's magazines such as *Open House* worked particularly hard to give their shows personality because, as the CBC's assistant supervisor of Talks and Public

Affairs explained, "women at home ... miss adult companionship, so we must try to bring them interesting people with stimulating and provocative ideas and information."[87]

Besides being good company for the folks at home, hosts and commentators were seen to give the shows a "distinctiveness and a unity which the printed magazine achieves through a distinctive writing style."[88] Hosts were thus presented as the *authors* and *animators* of the documentary text. Some appeared as authority figures: *Close-Up's* Frank Willis was "the great mover ... who summons the people, who brings them before our eyes and who makes them important ... all with a colossal assurance," according to the CBC radio program *Critically Speaking*. Others were more personable: *Tabloid's* crew acted as the cast of a "real life situation comedy," as producer Ross McLean put it.[89] Whatever the case, a personal approach was considered vital for audience involvement and ratings success. McLean reported "people taking up the cudgel for individual members of the cast, Percy Saltzman [getting] letters saying 'I like you but I don't like the others.'"[90] *Newsmagazine* claimed a 50 per cent ratings boost when it introduced a hosted format in the summer of 1956.[91]

This "subjectification" of Canadian documentary television was partly due to foreign influence, with Murrow and reporters like him as role models for journalists both north and south of the border. It was also a natural consequence of new production practices of television, the schedules often demanding a brief encounter between reporter and event, and nothing more.[92] But personalized programs were not merely technological accidents or encroachments of American show-biz values. Audience attachment to reporters and hosts was carefully cultivated in Canadian television just as it had been in Canadian radio. At the most basic level, documentary reporters were deliberately made more visible in the new shows. Ross McLean insisted on dispatching his "men" to the scene of the story to "develop in each reporter that TV standby, the familiar friend."[93] One McLean alumni, Percy Saltzman, reminded a reviewer of a "small boy trying to get into every picture," both in the studio and out in the field.[94] Moreover, producers used the TV cameras to achieve still deeper forms of identification, encouraging viewers to feel that they were actually accompanying reporters into the line of action. In a *Newsmagazine* feature on art schools, for instance, film crews mounted their cameras on toy wagons to convey a sense of motion, and then dangled out windows and lay "at dirt level" to give the impression of "going in there with [host] Harry [Rassky]."[95] Broadcasters thus carefully encouraged viewers to "delegate" their look to the reporter of the day.

Hosts were repositioned in the programs as *mediators* between the outside world and the home audience. "Cellomatic projectors" – rear screen projectors using transparent overlays – allowed hosts to interact with a variety of maps, graphs, and other icons, "connecting" with events in new ways.[96] Teleprompters, standard equipment on most sets by 1958, brought hosts closer to the audience by eliminating the "constant looking up from script to camera," thus allowing for more direct forms of address.[97] Announcer-hosts were transformed into more proximate figures of the documentary text, speaking "live" and direct to the audience from the newly constructed "intermediate" space of the studio.

A transcript of *Tabloid* host Dick Macdougal's introduction to a film feature on 4 October 1954 on the Hart House swimming pool in Toronto gives a further idea of the new role of the host:

DICK MACDOUGAL: Say, all this talk about warm weather has put me in the mood for a swim. [*Directly addresses the camera.*] How about you? Want to join me? ... Well, I'm going to take the plunge. I'll just walk over to the monitor ... [*Close-up on picture of Hart House pool.*]

Macdougal's introduction is notable for its directness and informality. As writer and critic Hugh Garner noted at the time, his "interesting, casual and amusing approach" stood in marked contrast to that of CBC news anchor Larry Henderson who generally "showed all the fire and enthusiasm of a guy telling his boss he was drunk the night before."[98] But more remarkable is Macdougal's *location* with respect to the story, from which he orchestrates the disparate spaces of the program into a more or less coherent text. As Garner noted, *Tabloid* was a "fantastic world" of scattered places and times, sometimes disorienting for the novice television viewer. But somehow Macdougal seemed to "make it all make sense."[99]

Another transcript from a 7 September 1957 edition of *Close-Up* further illustrates the new types of discursive work taken on by the host. "Our reporters [are] at the ready in *Close-Up*, a program designed to report and stimulate opinion," announces Frank Willis at the beginning of the program. His introduction of the first story follows: "And now, a public menace to us all, especially in the holiday season, which we at the CBC and this reporter in particular wanted to bring to you." The camera cuts to a shot of a man and his wife leaving a party, at which point Willis resumes his commentary:

FRANK WILLIS: The party had been routine. Drinking, music, lots of laughs. Leaving, his wife had suggested she'd better drive. He insisted he was all right. All right, maybe. Then a stop light. [*Close-up of a stop light passing by.*] Missed it. [*Shot of police car in pursuit, and then the man being pulled over.*] Then he was arrested. [*Shot of man being put in the car.*] Quietly, unspectacularly. This had never happened to him before ... [*Shot of man in police station.*] How much to drink? Only a beer? ... [*Shot of policeman mouthing words with Willis's voice-over.*]

Willis assumes a number of enunciative roles on which the coherency of this story depends. In narrative terms, he is both a diegetic and extradiegetic subject, appearing in the studio and from "within the story." He operates from a number of temporal and spatial positions ("And now a story," followed by "The party had been routine"). He speaks for the program (explaining *Close-Up*, its purpose, and its rules of discourse), for the network ("we at the CBC"), for the public (and the "menace to us all"), for himself ("this reporter in particular"), and finally for the characters in the story (there is no sync sound in this feature, and all the dialogue and thoughts of the characters are voiced by Willis). This is not to imply that Willis *was*, in fact, the author as well as the animator of these ideas and sentiments, although he did write most of his own introductions, as did many of his public affairs colleagues following the 1959 CBC producers strike.[100] But it is to say that by the late 1950s, programs such as *Close-Up* had created a new documentary subject on whom the trust and involvement of audiences was seen to depend.

DOCUMENTARY AND MODERN CULTURE

In short, in their first decade on the air, TV producers worked to make their documentaries more realistic and more entertaining, apparently making sense of Canadian life in a way that truly captured the imagination of a "general audience." Indeed, if we are to believe many producers and pundits at the time, the genre had remade itself into an up-to-date "modern" public service, delivering both clear and instructive meanings and responsible pleasures to viewers, albeit in ways policy-makers and educators had never dreamed of. Television, to paraphrase McLean, had made "facts" fun. It had effectively resolved the contradiction between pedagogy and pleasure in Canadian broadcasting. But a closer examination of the programs and the controversies surrounding them suggests that the relationship between documentary, television, and official modern culture was in fact much more complex than such an account would indicate.

Crucially, documentary television seemed incapable of maintaining established public service hierarchies of knowledge and representation, especially the traditional priority in Canada of information over entertainment. "Middle ground" information shows were particularly problematic in this respect because of the way they blurred the boundaries between fact and fiction. *Tabloid*, the CBC's first English-language magazine program, was a case in point, receiving stories from six different information and entertainment departments "in all manner of styles," covering everything from "farm topics, sports, public affairs and cultural highbrow matters."[101] Most stories were developed in consultation with the CBC's newly developed Audience Research Department and then given a good deal of show-biz publicity in newspapers and trade magazines before being inserted between the national newscast and CBC's prime time entertainment lineup. In short, *Tabloid* was produced, promoted, and scheduled in ways increasingly indistinct from entertainment television.

Genre bending was a subject of much concern at the CBC. Public affairs supervisors closely monitored *Tabloid*'s progress and its influence on other forms of information programming. And while they generally commended the show for its "informality and strong appeal through wisecracking," they worried that "in the long run. these [approaches] might have an influence on the news" and other programs.[102] The chief news editor cited efforts by news anchor Larry Henderson "to personalize his newscast, by reporting news which he had gathered and crediting himself with the report" – an early effort at public affairs-type "hosting" that supervisors hoped to nip in the bud "once and for all."[103] In the end the CBC opted for a "divorce" between news and public affairs programming, by introducing a clearer break between *Tabloid* and the newscast, and hiring two separate announcers in late 1953.[104]

But the network still had problems determining where information left off and entertainment took over. For instance, finding a proper documentary mode of address was very problematic. In 1954 CBC chair Davidson Dunton noted the practice of using first names in documentary and public affairs interviews, which he thought to be of "questionable taste [and] ... more acceptable in sports interviews."[105] Flagrant commercialism was an even greater cause for concern. Supervisors worried about the rising level of advertising in magazine stories, one editor counting a "total of six plugs" in a five-minute feature film on *Tabloid*.[106] Maintaining generic boundaries and the priority of information seemed to require constant vigilance.

But first names and brand names proved easier to control than more subtle presentational styles. *Newsmagazine* in 1954 was seen by some supervisors to have exceeded its "straight reporting mandate" by featuring stories which were "opinionated and of a controversial character ... which should properly be considered in separate programs."[107] The cultural magazine *Quest* was similarly criticized for mixing documentary with drama by inserting actuality shots into its fictional scripts. One disapproving consultant noted that a policy forbidding the use of "the documentary technique except in genuine documentaries" would be difficult to enforce because the Corporation had not traditionally distinguished between these two program types.[108]

The boundary between information and entertainment became even less clear in the early part of television's second decade, as producers began to question the more "objective" conventions of documentary discourse. With regard to interviewing, some supported the corporate line that the "interviewer's personality remain completely in the background," while others such as Douglas Leiterman argued for a more flamboyant "devil's advocate role."[109] Many supervisors found the latter approach "personal, pointed and rude," but it nonetheless became a mainstay of shows like *This Hour Has Seven Days*.[110]

To some extent these experiments – and the increasing generic confusion which accompanied them – were the result of a growing "collective restlessness" on the part of Canadian documentary producers. As Robert Fulford noted in 1963, producer roles and program boundaries were all up for grabs in the wake of the recent CBC producers' strike.[111] At the same time, boundaries were hard to maintain because of new broadcast market conditions, the CBC coming under enormous commercial pressures in the early 1960s to further popularize documentary, sometimes at the expense of traditional pedagogical principles. Even general interest shows were in something of a ratings slump. In October 1963 the most widely viewed CBC documentary program, *The Nature of Things*, reached only 896,000 Canadian homes, while *Close-Up's* audience had fallen to under 600,000, a small number by the standards of the day.[112] Not one of the CBC's public affairs shows was left in its 8 to 10 p.m. "prime" prime-time schedule by 1963. In short, documentary and public affairs audiences were considered smaller than they needed to be, especially as the CBC began competing with the new CTV network and a growing number of private affiliates carrying U.S. programs. "After 11 years of operation, without any competition in most places," noted *Toronto Star* critic Nathan Cohen in September 1963, "CBC public affairs programming has by its own admission less of a hold than ever on its viewers."[113]

In these circumstances, public affairs producers began reinventing the documentary form – further calling into question the very purpose and identity of public affairs television in Canada.[114] *This Hour Has Seven Days* worked at making its documentary inserts shorter, generally no more than six minutes, and freely mixing them with satirical sketches, live remotes, and more aggressive studio interviews. Producers partly credited the new format for a dramatic increase in the ratings of the show, which reached an estimated audience of 3.3 million Canadians on 3 May 1966. This was half the total audience for English Canada at that hour, and the biggest audience for any Canadian program other than *Hockey Night in Canada*.[115] But this new faster-paced hybrid format clearly offered something other than "public information" as traditionally conceived in Canada.[116] The increasing confusion between information and entertainment called into question not just the boundaries of a particular genre but the nature and distinctiveness of Canadian public service television. As one reviewer remarked, "this [*Seven Days*] makes me wonder if we're not just airing our own brand of American television."[117]

New forms of "sensationalism" further cast doubts on the integrity of public service broadcasting and documentary television in particular. This highly politicized term had a number of connotations in the 1960s. Sometimes it meant documentary showmanship, or what one critic called the "staging of stunts at the expense of responsible reporting."[118] Hidden cameras, ambush interviews, and "muckraking," either in the public or private sphere, were the tools of this trade.[119] What concerned the critics was not just the racy topics nor the graphic footage, nor even the supposedly "unbalanced" and partisan nature of the shows; just as problematic was the uncertain line they drew between "documentation" and "provocation." Many documentary programs were seen to rest on an increasingly uncertain epistemological foundation, with stories being "made" rather than "covered." Documentary television had become "part" of what it was meant to be "about." The new wave of documentary and public affairs shows thus called into question the ability of public service television to make sense of Canada in a detached way – one that maintained the integrity of both documentary programming and its subject matter. Again the distinction between fact and fiction on Canadian television had become increasingly blurred.

"Sensationalism" also referred to television's confusion of right and wrong – that is, to its inability to "distinguish between the normal and the abnormal, the acceptable and the unacceptable."[120] Early documentary reports on homosexuality were a case in point. *Close-Up* had been criticized in 1958 for sensation seeking and superficiality in its pioneering five-minute portrait of an anonymous London doctor in which host Frank Willis had declared gay lifestyle to be a "large and complicated issue, [for which] this report is submitted in no sense as a conclusive comment." Declared one reviewer, "Brief chats with furtive types hardly add to our knowledge of this way of life."[121] CBC *Sunday*'s "follow-up report" nearly ten years later, on the other hand, sought to provide a more indepth report, including interviews with gay men and transsexuals, a filmed report on San Francisco's Castro District, and an "inside look" at Montreal's Hawaiian Club. Broadcast in early 1967, "The Gay Life" was similarly castigated for a lack of moral authority, one CBC official noting the program's inability to "hold within what the majority of our viewers consider standards of taste."[122] The program received complaints from at least five CBC affiliates across the country, while supervisors at network headquarters noted the show's failure to avail itself of "whatever Canadian (psychiatric and psychological) expertise is available in this difficult and sensitive area."[123] Overall, producers were accused of seeking publicity and ratings at the expense of authoritative and responsible programming.

Arts documentaries seemed even less capable of settling matters of cultural distinction. The "far from highbrow" attempt in 1961 by the *Lively Arts* to investigate "what makes artists work, what they get out of it," and to determine by panel discussion "what is good taste," was deemed "stupid and frivolous" by a number of critics,[124] as was an attempt by *The Nature of Things* to distinguish "where science leaves off and fiction begins" (in a 1960 program examining the arguments of a man who said he had been to Venus, and a scientist who talked to dolphins.)[125] Canada's new wave of documentary reporters lacked the authority to make such judgments, many critics implied, because they were neither representative of the public, sheltered as they were in their Toronto studios, nor accredited experts, hired as most of them had been without any post-secondary education. In short, documentary programming seemed unable as an institution to arbitrate between competing knowledge claims concerning Canadian society, and unable or unwilling to offer convincing credible alternative accounts of its own. In these conditions, critical documentary reports were seen to amount to nothing more than "debunking" and "grandstanding."[126]

For other critics, the *form* and not just the *content* of documentary programs was becoming increasingly problematic. Semiotic and narrative conventions – the use of sights, sounds, and stories in documentary reports – had originally been rather rigid in Canada, with technical journals such as *Radio* acknowledging the need for dissolves, fades, and rapid transitions in exceptional circumstances, while frowning upon jump cuts and any sort of "gimmickry" to lend vitality to shows.[127] Jump cuts should always be avoided, film editor Harold Wright had advised in the early 1950s, because they might make "the interview subject's head spin around, making the viewer lose orientation." He recommended instead a broad use of close-ups and simple designs, since they alone would not "tax the eyes of the viewers" of a limited-resolution TV screen.[128] Graphics should be "pleasing to the eye – but they must never obtrude themselves on the observer ... they must never detract or compete with the story," according to *Tabloid* producer Jack Kruper in 1956.[129] With respect to sound, producers were advised to seek out appropriate ambient noises in lieu of the more remote non-sync narrations of Canadian documentary films; excessive multi-track recording, however, was discouraged due to receiver limitations, as were sounds that could not be immediately identified and matched with the stripped-down images on the screen.[130] Music should help guide the viewer through the narrative structure of the show, serving as a bridge between story items, between stories and commercials, between opening and closing segments and the body of the show, and between the constantly juxtaposed "live" studio and (usually) recorded location sites of television actuality.[131] Constant collaboration was recommended to ensure that these various levels of signification worked together to produce coherent messages and predictable pleasures. All in all, the signs and symbols of documentary television were expected to *mean* something to viewers.

By some accounts, images, sounds, and graphics worked just this way. Critic Marion Lepkin praised the documentary program *Explorations* for "really using the medium ... [with] cartoons, lectures and film clips and dramatic skits and graphs ... in short everything but the kitchen sink, but all of a piece, with not a rag or a tatter anywhere."[132] At the same time, even in the early 1950s, critics and producers themselves had worried that this new razzmatazz world of multiplying signifiers and diegetic fields might not always make sense. Some degree of "confusion" was to be expected, visiting American producer Gilbert Seldes had pointed out. The best that producers could hope for was a sort of low-key engagement, and programs should try to stimulate the audience without inducing techno-fatigue or even schizoid dissociation.[133] Many critics called for more narrative and semiotic supervision at the CBC, to make sure the programs avoided just that effect. Miriam Waddington, writing in the *Canadian Forum* in 1956, complained that images and sounds were too often straying from a linear, educational path with "words pulling one way and pictures another."[134] The CBC's own technical officer complained that editing in the programs was often "deplorable ... inject[ing] synthetic action into shows by a series of unmotivated cuts."[135] Similarly the corporation's National Program Office noted that graphics "often competed with stories" and that scripts were often "devoid of any logic" other than building a bridge between images and commercials.[136]

But semiotic excess only increased in documentary television's second decade, with a new generation of producers advocating a post-literate and post-cinematic model of documentary programming that stressed images and spectacle over words, messages, and conventional expository structures. Producers Patrick Watson and Douglas Leiterman cited with approval Marshall McLuhan's idea of television as an "acoustic space" where images, sounds, and graphics could flood the senses and overwhelm strictly linear meanings.[137] While *Inquiry, This Hour Has Seven Days*, and *Document* hardly "unleashed signs" and "relinquished sense" in this way, their producers clearly worked to offer not just information but a new sensual experience as part of the package.

Even if producers never put their new theories into practice, critics worried that meaning might be lost in whatever new documentary mix emerged. Radical new editorial practices, for instance, threatened to undermine both the linear sense of the shows and the empirical authority on which they rested. *This Hour Has Seven Days*, for instance, popularized a form of deconstructive montage in which the show's own footage regarding what was "really happening" in Canada was contrasted with obviously suspect government information films. Some critics charged that such ironic juxtapositions threatened to make *all* documentary accounts suspect and strip all TV images of their indexical overtones. "You can't believe anyone or anything anymore … that's the *Seven Days* message," concluded one reviewer.[138] Transparent "arty" editing practices seemed to further diminish the linearity and indexical force of the programs. *Inquiry* used jarring jump cuts and special effects to poke fun at social and political conventions, inserting "out of nowhere, for no discernible reason," according to one critic, an animated graphic of the Peace Tower exploding in a 1963 story on Canadian defence policy.[139] Less experimentally but more controversially, *This Hour Has Seven Days* introduced "transparent" editing to its interview features – that is, flagrantly manipulated footage, subject to higher shooting ratios and cutting rates, which the show's producers saw as a more compelling form of actuality. For many critics, documentary editing had reached a point where keeping faith with the viewer – delivering an unaltered account of Canadian life – had been sacrificed to the cause of generating excitement. *Seven Days*, in this view, offered "lots of action but not much real information."[140]

But that was not all. Documentary programming was further seen to undermine Canadian television's pedagogical project by failing to regulate its *pleasures*. The ways whereby audiences were encouraged to identify with hosts and involve themselves in programming seemed distinctly at odds with the rational citizen-building projects advocated by the Massey Commission. *Newsmagazine*'s Harry Rassky told revealing story in 1953 about a viewer giving him a hug outside his Toronto studio for having "captured" the then notorious Boyd Gang: "Somehow the fact that I was the one who brought the story vividly into her living room was confused with the actual arrest."[141] Apocryphal or not, such stories indicated the degree to which producers expected and sometimes encouraged non-pedagogical (and cognitively confused) forms of audience identification. The continued ratings success of graphic and visually involving programs such as *Seven Days, Sunday,* and even CTV's W5 confirmed critics's fears that viewers' "most immature and masochistic desires" were being being indulged at the expense of any gains in knowledge.[142] Alas, documentary programs were being watched and enjoyed for all the wrong reasons.

WOMEN'S MAGAZINE SHOWS

Sensationalism, genre bending, the unleashing of audiovisual signs in an attempt to please or excite the viewer all represented for many critics in the 1950s and '60s documentary television's dangerous slide into excess. And women's magazine shows symbolized the very worst the genre had to offer. These were introduced to Canadian television in 1954, partly because of complaints from cultural critics about soap operas and partly because of demands from advertisers for new types of commercially oriented women's programming. Early on, programmers felt women would have no time to watch TV during the day. But the success of American daytime magazines such as NBC's *Today* show made them think again: "Only lack of studio facilities [prevented] the CBC from scheduling similar programs."[143] The corporation hoped the Canadian homemaker would soon "learn to plan her day around her set." Information programming would do its part to relieve the boredom and loneliness of domestic life, introducing women to "interesting people with stimulating provocative ideas and information."[144]

Women's programming did bring entirely new subjects and styles to documentary television. In the early 1950s, *Living* introduced regular film features on fashion, gardening, home decoration, and hobbies in an "accessible fashion."[145] *Place aux dames* and *Pour elle* on the French network mixed "women's reports" with songs and variety sketches.[146] On the English network, *Open House* and later *Take 30* covered everything from "cooking to sexuality to international affairs" in a "personable and direct way."[147] The work of Jo Kowin, a producer and editor for *Open House* and *Explorations*, was particularly influential in the early years of the genre, introducing a non-realist approach to documentary that was dubbed "thought-sync" programming. Using audiovisual tracks to express the inner feelings of her subjects, Kowin offered a collage of symbolic and metaphorical sounds and images in the 1956 *Explorations* feature "The Unseeing Eye," a program about the sensual experiences of blind people.[148]

For some observers, women's shows were a welcome if marginal addition to documentary television. Ohio University awarded its "special interest group award" to *Open House*, citing its "mood-evoking use of intimate camera and restrained commentary," a style that was assumed to be "unusually appealing for housewives."[149] But in Canada the programs were the subject of an unusual amount of derision in the press. Critics complained of their "frenetic pace": "Eight minutes of this, 10 minutes of that ... is women's attention really so short?" asked one reviewer in 1953.[150] Others castigated the shows for "flagrant commercialism," noting the frequency of "self-promotional inserts to keep viewers glued to the set."[151] Some columnists worried that such new modes of representation effectively feminized and degraded Canadian television as a public sphere: "By the time these programs are finished," commented one reviewer, "everyone with a TV set is reduced to a mass of quivering sentimental jelly."[152] New rules of representation thus called into question the most basic (gendered) distinctions on which public service broadcasting was seen to rest in Canada: distinctions between pedagogy and pleasure, between culture and commerce, and, of course, between public and private affairs.

AN EXAMPLE: "SCHIZOPHRENIA"

Controversies surrounding the form and content of documentary programming were not limited to the popular magazine shows, however. A textual analysis of the educational program *Explorations* and one of its documentary features concerning mental illness gives us an idea of the narrative and semiotic practices prevailing in other areas of documentary programming and allows us to assess more fully Canadian television's ability and commitment to make sense of its world in the "golden age" of public service broadcasting.

Explorations was launched in October 1956 and promoted as the CBC's "boldest venture to date in the documentary field."[153] The program was designed to tackle a wide range of subjects to do with "society, its origins and the physical world," and promised to use a number of techniques to tackle these issues including filmed documentaries, dramas, and discussion. This was emphatically not a magazine series. Program planners stressed that their features would not be limited by time restrictions; if a story could not be dealt with in an hour (more time than was allotted to documentary features almost anywhere else on television), it would simply be continued the next week. Further, each feature was to have its own experienced guide rather than a regular program host, and the show pledged to tackle difficult documentary subjects not often dealt with by broadcasters. Program topics for the first season included a study of Canadian theatres in the nineteenth century and an item entitled "Love in Tin Pan Alley," which took a "detached look at lyrics of a pop song with the help of social semanticist S.I. Hayakawa."[154] *Explorations* thus became noted for its comprehensive and often experimental approach to topics that "other public affairs producers wouldn't touch."[155] This, it seemed, was the documentary program educators had always dreamed of.

In early 1958 *Explorations* began preparing a program about schizophrenia. Mental health had been a recurring concern of the program in its first years on the air, and producers had cooperated quite extensively with the Canadian Mental Health Association in earlier productions. The "Schizophrenia" program was produced by Felix Lazarus of CBC Winnipeg and written by Evelyn Cherry and Sidney Katz in cooperation with Humphrey Osmond, a psychiatrist at the University of Saskatchewan. The aim of all concerned was to make a program that "explored a hidden area of human experience" in a meaningful but "non-institutional way."[156]

Broadcast on 29 January 1959, the program begins with an image of a hospital facade, followed by a number of shots of patients in the hallways inside. "One in twelve of us will spend part of our lives in a place such as this," the narrator announces. "Nearly a million patients, because of illnesses of mind rather than body, are locked away in such great fortresses dotted across the country." The narrator continues with more national statistics, and then notes that scientists at Saskatchewan Mental Hospital in Wayburn are working towards a "cure." "The moving spirit behind this work is Dr Humphrey Osmond," we are told, as the camera cuts to a close-up of a young man and his parents pulling up to the hospital gate. At this point Osmond takes over the narration, providing still more statistics about mental illness around the country, then turning his attention to the family arriving at the hospital. "Poor bewildered parents," Dr Osmond intones: "Their son has been changing gradually, withdrawing first from society around him and then from the family, until finally in desperation they are forced to seek help, to come to this place of strange people and monstrous crazy house associations. 'Is this the place of no return?'" Osmond imagines them asking. "'Will our son spend the rest of his life here'"?

These remarks are accompanied by a close-up of the patient's first hesitant steps up the hospital stairs. At this point discordant music takes over the soundtrack. The music continues as patient and family approach the admissions desk. "Yet I believe for them and their John, there has never been as much hope," Osmond insists. "New chemicals allow us to experience some of the mental anguish of the schizophrenia patient, to some extent to put ourselves in his shoes for a few hours."

The program continues with a shot of John being escorted down a hallway by a nurse. "We know that John is acutely aware of his surrounding, the reception centre, the strange people," explains Osmond. The camera then cuts to a shot of a dramatically lit door, followed by a close-up of a key being inserted, and then an animated sequence of a dungeon gate and sound effects of distant slamming doors. "Poor John," notes Osmond, "thrown into a state of hallucination as the trap seems to close in upon him. In Saskatchewan, with funding from federal and provincial treasuries, we've been working to prove a theory ..."

Osmond elaborates on his theory that schizophrenics suffer from a chemical imbalance in the brain that can be simulated with the use of a drug called adrenochrome, and d-lysergic acid (LSD-25):

We had to take this stuff ourselves to test its effect. [*Cut to shot of confused looking scientist in lab coat.*] After inhaling the drug, my colleague Dr Hoffer becomes suspicious of everyone. [*Cut to shot of an inhaler lying on top of an academic paper authored by Hoffer.*] It took him half an hour to choose between tea and coffee. [*Cut to shot of Osmond taking notes as Hoffer looks at tea and coffee cups in front of him in confusion.*] Anxiety rose and he thought he'd better quit his job.

Osmond then goes on to describe his own experiences with the drug, which he claims to have taken fifteen times in the last year, noting that for him "these episodes have been among the most strange, most awesome and, in their own way, the most beautiful in my life."

At this point the truly hallucinatory part of the program begins, with a number of seemingly disconnected images proceeding in rapid procession. Osmond the narrator explains that after taking LSD, "a special sense of significance invests everything around me." His words are accompanied by a close-up of a flower casting a shadow on the wall. "If I fix my attention on the flower, I could spend all day contemplating it." The program proceeds with Osmond's reflections on (in order of their appearance) leaves, chairs, faces in windows, grains of wood, and the resemblances of doors to coffins – all accompanied by suitably stylized graphics. The segment then builds to a whirling surreal climax. Osmond continues:

I asked for a glass of water and noticed it tasted strange. Poison crossed my mind, and the story of Socrates and hemlock. And almost at the same moment a calculation by a physicist who claimed that every glass of water contains an atom of Socrates. [*Close-up of water going down the drain.*] I looked into the water, and in its swirling depths was a vortex [*close-up of vortex*] which went down into the centre of the world. My companions then dragged me away from the glass of water.

The camera then cuts to a shot of Osmond back in his lab coat in his office, directly addressing the camera. "Already we have learned enough from accounts like these to make progress fighting the disease," he notes, concluding with a last look at John, and the efforts going on across the country to treat the illness.

"Schizophrenia" is an unusual program by any measure but a truly remarkable one given the context in which it appeared. Television had come a long way from the institutional approach of the National Film Board era, when subjects such as these were tackled as macrosocial issues to be explained in a detached impersonal manner. *Explorations*'s personal and free-form investigation is largely at odds both with documentary as such and with early policy visions of the genre as a linear and sensible service avoiding all "facile theatrical effects."[157] Clearly even in its most educational venues, television had come of age as a documentary service in ways quite unforeseen in its founding pedagogical charter.

"Schizophrenia," we should note, was more than just a personal treatment of a growing social problem, and more than an exercise in liberal empathy for the mentally ill. In fact, the program seems to subvert modernist regimes of representation at every turn, offering a free and often disorienting mix of indexical, iconic, and symbolic sights and sounds, in the form of a rapid alternation of institutional shots, hallucinatory graphics, expert commentary, and personal drugged-out ramblings. The program thus offers something of a "post-realist" television aesthetic which, just six short years after the inauguration of Canadian television service, was presumed to be both comprehensible and acceptable to the average viewer.

Also noteworthy is the program's unconventional editing, particularly its frequent reliance on forms of symbolic montage usually associated with fictional, dramatic, or avant-garde modes of expression. Not only does "Schizophrenia" offer public and private scenes in short order but the sequences often follow the logic of affect and inner feeling rather than that of physical causation in the outside world, the insertion of John's dungeon vision into the hospital admission segment being just one case in point. Insofar as it exists, continuity editing is clearly designed to express a form of disjointed personal experience and inner sensation rather than continuous time-space physical action per se. Music also serves as a bridge in this respect, matching hallucinations with the more "objective" institutional phases of the story. Here again the program works to erase distinctions between inner and outer space and between affect and reason – the epistemological distinctions on which documentary was founded as a public affairs genre in Canada.

Camera work similarly violates Canadian conventions of documentary realism, particularly of the Griersonian kind – designed as it is to *prevent* us from keeping our distance from the schizophrenic's world and thereby make sense of it in a responsible, institutional way. The constant juxtaposition of institutional and "inner world" perspectives, we might argue, works to strip both of their conventional connotations, with the former no longer remaining the "last word" concerning personal experience. Reason itself, in the person of Dr Osmond, constantly slips in and out of a coherent state, the program thus breaking down not just conventional oppositions between "public" and "private" and the "institutional" and the "personal" but the ability of these binaries to make sense of schizophrenia in any lasting or authoritative way. Schizophrenia, as Osmond himself notes, is a "many-sided issue."

Finally, the program seems designed to offer something more than conventional realist pleasures. By shifting topics and modes of address at such a pace, it seems designed to appeal not just to our desire for knowledge – the ostensible purpose of documentary programming in its founding public service charter – but to our sensuous pleasure in gazing, to our willingness to enter a new and fantastic realm of experience. In Freudian terms, the program appeals to our sense of scopophilia as well as epistophelia.

In short, "Schizophrenia" can be seen as a case study of public service broadcasting's failure to "make sense" of an emerging social problem in an orderly pedagogical way. In "Schizophrenia" we see the inability or unwillingness of Canada's public service broadcaster to regulate the meanings and pleasures of television in line with the nation's ostensible postwar cultural objectives. Even in its purest educational moments, then, documentary television arguably failed to function as an authoritative "modern" public service.

CONCLUSION

So what does this tell us about public service broadcasting as a modern project in Canada? One might argue not much. We could dismiss the "middle ground" experiment as mere neo-paternalism, as plain old public service broadcasting with a show-biz veneer, born out of a desperation to keep American commercial television at bay. And we could argue, as have many researchers, that pleasure always remained instrumental to Canadian television's pedagogical project. In short, we could conclude that whatever its allowance for new modes of address and new opportunities for audience identification, Canadian television remained dedicated in the end to the task of using sounds and images to make sense of *all* aspects of Canadian life for *all* Canadians in more or less predictable ways. Such a view probably fairly sums up the hopes of the original architects of Canada's public service television service.

But clearly the "middle ground" experiment was never so neat and easily contained as that. Canadian television never seemed able to contain all meanings and pleasures within fixed liberal-patriarchal boundaries. Nor did it manage to consistently and effectively police its own semiotic systems, harnessing images, sounds and graphics to the logic of the written word. Nor, finally, did it successfully maintain a modernist set of distinctions between pedagogy and pleasure, between the sensational and the sublime, and between ostensibly public and private modes of representation. In short, in its defining genre, and even in its "golden age," Canadian television consistently fell short of its own high modernist ideals.

Of course, Canadian public service broadcasting may have been exceptional in this regard. Canada's "middle ground" television may have been a natural site for what Lynn Spigel in another context has called the "queering" of the semiotic protocols and the epistemological and moral boundaries of modernist television.[158] My point, however, one that I will return to in the chapters that follow, is simply that the monolithic periodization that has come to dominate European and American media histories, based on a clear divide between modern (national public service) and postmodern (global commercial) television,[159] does not really apply in the Canadian case. Here at least – and perhaps elsewhere? – the relationship between national public service television and modernity was far from clear cut.

4 Documentary Television as a National Project, 1965–90

In the mid-1960s documentary television in Canada underwent two major changes. First, it was regulated like never before, as television executives sought to curb what they saw to be the discursive "excesses" of the previous decade. And second (and relatedly) it found itself incorporated within a wider attempt broadcasters to document – systematically and reliably – the various times and spaces of the nation. This new era, which continued well into the 1980s, was in terms of regulatory ambition and stylistic sweep the height of Canadian television's documentary national project.

This chapter examines strategies of representation that emerged at this time, focusing on four core areas: vérité programs, long-form documentary "essays," docudramas, and journalistic reports. I begin with a study of perhaps the most perennially controversial form, vérité programming, and the problems it encountered representing the nation to itself.

VÉRITÉ PROGRAMS

Vérité television in Canada was designed to present a natural and intimate portrait of everyday life, allowing subjects to speak for themselves free of journalistic mediation. But like its counterparts in other countries,[1] the Canadian genre largely failed to live up to this naturalistic ideal. To begin with, Canadian television never managed to reflect Canadian life without interruption or mediation. Vérité programs were almost invariably broken up by commercials, and almost always more tightly edited than their filmic counterparts (because of the supposedly shorter attention spans and more casual interests of home viewers). Journalistic commentary was also the rule and not the exception, especially in series productions where stories were positioned and made sense of within regular line-ups, but also in stand-alone features where even self-styled vérité purists such as Allan King frequently resorted to at least limited narration to "put viewers in the picture [before] leaving them alone with the subject."[2] Interviews were also a common feature of the form and never, as Ross McLean warned against in the late 1960s, allowed to become a "forgotten art in the search for new [more naturalistic] documentary styles."[3] Vérité was thus a bastard form on Canadian television, more obviously edited and embellished than its filmic counterpart but still quite distinct from other forms of documentary television with regard to its standards of authenticity.

Canada's first vérité program was typically both a compromise and an innovation of documentary form. *Skid Row*, Allan King's 1956 portrait of vagrants and alcoholics in downtown Vancouver, relying on narration, music, and reenactments to tell its stories, was hardly an unvarnished picture of Canadian street life. But it was still rightfully seen as a unique achievement for Canadian television in terms of both subject and style; homeless people had never appeared on Canadian TV before, at least not for long, in a documentary format where they seemed to be going about their business in more or less spontaneous ways. King's subjects spoke at length, for up to two minutes at a time, an unprecedented occurrence on Canadian television in the 1950s, only infrequently interrupted by the director's own whimsical reflections on the meaning of their lives. They also took King and his viewers on a unique tour of their various routines, from the hymn sings at the Salvation Army to the rubbing-alcohol parties in the alleys next door. In these ways at least, *Skid Row* showed new sides of Canadian life in new ways.

Subsequent vérité productions used a wider range of *interview techniques* and *recording technologies* to get closer to Canadian life. Vérité producers were of course filmmakers, but they were also ethnographers, using charm and stealth to elicit natural behaviour from their subjects. King himself relied on "old-fashioned rapport" to extract a series of wrenching confessionals for the 1958 feature *A Matter of Pride*, producing the first genuine tears seen on Canadian television.[4] Others, such as *Candid Eye*'s Tom Daly, resorted to multiple camera techniques so that subjects were never aware when and from where they were being filmed. The producers of the 1959 documentary special *National Survival*, a vérité portrait of life in a bomb shelter, used observation windows through which volunteer subjects never saw the crews filming them.[5]

English-language productions were especially ruthless in their efforts to coax candid behaviour from their subjects. Some simply never bothered with the ethical protocols (and moments of self-reflection) evident in the work of Quebecois counterparts such as Michel Brault and Pierre Perrault. This difference of approach resulted in different forms of "vérité truth" on English and French television, as Brian Winston has noted, with the actuality of the former seen to be guaranteed by the rapport filmmakers established with their subjects off-camera, and that of the latter by the audience's ability to "keep an eye" on filmmakers in a work in progress.[6] But in each case, truth was seen to derive in large part from the "ethnographic" abilities (however these were conceived) of the producer. As critic Stanley Kauffman noted in a review of Allan King's work, what vérité producers needed most were "interpersonal skills" because even the most powerful filmmaker alive would be "powerless to make these films without the confidence of his subjects."[7]

These intangible personal skills were important assets for vérité producers, because they had to deal intimately with their subjects, relatively unbound by the conventional guidelines of documentary journalism. Non-series features in particular tended to be produced by independent companies such as Allan King and Associates, and produced by two to three person crews which often "made up the rules" as they went along, as one CBC supervisor testily put it.[8] In the early years of vérité production, there was no television formula per se for investigating private life (although, as we shall see, a number of journalistic policy books subsequently tried to provide one) and vérité investigations remained to a large extent an individual empathic exercise.[9] At least in its early years, then, Canadian vérité production was the closest documentary television ever got to an auteur tradition.

But beyond its personal insights, vérité television was seen to yield harder empirical truths which came with technological guarantees.

Producers and technicians developed a number of instruments in the mid-1960s with which to "faithfully" (and irrefutably) record everyday life. Light audio-visual kits and remote wireless camera units, developed for the royal visit of 1959, allowed documentary reporters to wade into a number of public and private events, such as the behind-the-scenes lobbying of the 1962 federal election campaign shown in Douglas Leiterman's 1962 "The Servant of All: Anatomy of an Election" for the program *Document*. Sixteen-millimetre sync sound cameras, originally developed at the NFB for *Lonely Boy*, a 1961 portrait of pop singer Paul Anka, allowed for quieter and less obtusive portrayals of private life and also more searching looks due to the wider range of lenses that were coming into use. New video cameras were also *cheaper* to use and more suited to natural light shooting, allowing for longer takes, easier edits, and wider coverage of hitherto unexplored social areas. Family squabbles, behind-the-scenes power broking, alternative life-styles, and even the nation's new "swinging" nightlife now came within documentary television's purview.

To be sure, recording technologies were not always up to the task. Producer frustration with the new equipment was evident well into the 1960s. Bolex cameras lacked adequate zoom and focus features, auricon units were found to be comfortable and light-weight but noisy, and none of the equipment was as invisible as producers sometimes claimed. Douglas Leiterman bragged that Liberal candidate Lester B. Pearson was so unaware of CBC cameras during the 1962 election that he actually bit into a microphone instead of a doughnut at a garden party. Leiterman also admitted that politicians were developing a sixth sense by which they could detect even the faintest "clacking of the camera above the din," a sense no doubt helped along by the half ton of recording equipment CBC crews were generally lugging around to these events at the time.[10] Nonetheless, the new technologies were seen to record and not merely interpret hidden areas of Canadian life, yielding direct filmic accounts with a precision and fidelity that could scarcely be questioned as documentary evidence.

Native charm and better technologies were believed to produce not just more realistic shows but more *involving* television. Portable, "silent" cameras were seen to allow filmmakers to follow various threads of subjects' private lives and develop more personal narratives with which viewers could identify in more emotional ways. The more compact equipment, as Leiterman noted, permitted stories to be covered from "tighter and different angles," encouraging new and more intimate forms of viewer involvement with characters on screen.[11]

But for all its impressive technology and radical new protocols, vérité television was problematic even for its fiercist advocates. First of all, programmers worried the new productions simply *didn't make sense*. They feared that without any obvious narrative structures or guiding commentaries, and relying on dim lighting and often muffled sounds, these everyday life stories were hard to follow. To be sure, producers attempted to develop an implicit new "screen language" to compensate for vérité's fuzzier aspects. Directors such as Allan King, Richard Ballantyne, and Beryll Fox learned to make up for the missing voice-over explanations by picking familiar subjects for their work. This partially accounts for the prominence of party leaders and public figures in the early productions. Editors tried to make up for the lack of viewer guidance by stressing time-space continuity, or as Aarla Saare put it, "simplicity and rhythm" rather than smart-alecky showy cuts."[12] Camera operators learned to focus on the narratively important aspects of events and subjects, or as Allan King said, "to lock into a scene in a totally intuitive way and just go with it."[13] Vérité crews also tended to immerse themselves in their subject matter more than their conventional documentary colleagues, so that they could focus on guiding themes once productions got under way.

But even as they went out of their way to impose documentary order on the flux of Canadian life, programmers still worried that the "natural" images of vérité would be more or less unmanageable, and indecipherable, on the small screen. Richard Ballantyne's *Mr Pearson* (1962) was not shown on television until 1969, not just because of its subject's rough language, but because of its "appalling technical quality," as CBC president Alphonse Ouimet put it.[14] They were also concerned that vérité's lengthy takes would not easily allow for commercial breaks. Moreover, they wondered if vérité was entertaining enough. Producers in the 1960s worked to make their stories less austere, borrowing a good many narrative tricks from fictional television, particularly soap operas. Programs featured intimate close-ups and scenes in which the compression of time was minimal (or at least well-hidden). Allan King's *A Married*

Couple (1969) essentially consisted of multiple plotlines and scenes rearranged for emotional impact.[15] King described his programs as "actuality dramas," working spontaneous action into dramatic form in order to explore personal experience.[16] In the sense that they promised dramatic "slices" of everyday life, vérité productions were regarded as art as well as actuality. But for all the genre's similarities with fiction, network officials still believed it had a long way to go as entertainment. The dramatic payoffs of most vérité shows, according to one CBC supervisor, were simply too "few and far between."[17]

Some were convinced that even if audiences were watching, it was for the wrong reasons. It was not just that programs dealt with private rather than "serious" public matters; they did so in a style which seemed to disallow any analytic detachment or proper documentary disposition on the part of viewers. Again the spectre of the undisciplined audience reared its head for Canadian television critics. "What do we learn from watching kids up close die before our eyes?" asked one reviewer.[18] The shows were "voyeurism plain and simple," noted another,[19] whose sentiments echoed those of cultural authorities regarding magazine stories in earlier years (see chapter 3). Vérité television seemed to offer the pleasures of *gazing* rather than the virtues of *knowing*.

Still other critics were concerned about the effects of the programs on their subjects as well as their audiences. In 1957 the CBC was able to argue that programs such as *Skid Row* allowed their subjects "dignity and a chance for self-discovery" and further informed their viewers about "the extent of misery and suffering at Vancouver's back door."[20] Early features like *Skid Row* were often accompanied by "solution pieces" showing steps that were being taken to help the subjects portrayed in the program. Similarly, home movies on *The Way It Is* and like-minded series in the late 1960s were characterized as therapeutic for their makers and instructive for their viewers, saying "more about what it is happening in Canadian society than a stack of textbooks."[21] Vérité productions could thus be held up as benefiting both subjects and society at large, opening up hidden dysfunctional spaces for inspection and (self-) regulation.

The "social benefits" of later programs were less clear, however. Critics noted the genre's "relentless proccupation with the sordid."[22] They also questioned the ethics of productions such as Tanya

Ballantyne's 1967 NFB film *The Things I Cannot Change*, which after its airing on CBC Television was accused of betraying the trust of its subjects and exploiting their images.[23] Others pointed out the large numbers of films about women, ethnic minorities, and low income groups, who tended to be depicted as "social problems to be scrutinized" rather than people deserving of representation.[24]

Journalists tended to defend the new investigative techniques not because they were right but because they were inevitable. "Increasingly for better or worse," noted Douglas Leiterman, "there are experiences which omnipresent cameras record and transmission towers relay across the country."[25] Jocelyn Dingon asked, "what are we doing in these people's kitchens with our lights, our cameras, and our microphones," noting that television's approaches to low income people in particular had taken on the "unfortunate air of tourism."[26] Television officials found even this "reluctant panopticon" defence unconvincing and unacceptable. "The one thing we will work to improve," noted CBC president Alphonse Ouimet in the wake of the "Youth and Morality" program, "is our method of collecting information," The implication was clear that vérité television's new surveillance technologies could and would be reined in.[27]

Restrictions were in fact soon brought into effect by Canada's public and private broadcasters, introducing a chilling effect on the genre as a whole. In the late 1960s, the CBC's journalistic policy books specified the conditions under which profanity, nudity, and sexuality could be depicted.[28] The use of clandestine equipment such as hidden cameras or microphones was forbidden as a "general rule," and only permitted in the "public interest."[29] Individuals' rights to privacy could only be breached when their private lives became a matter of legitimate concern. Similarly, if more noncommitally, the CTV Code of Ethics promised a "respect for the dignity and privacy of everyone with whom we deal."[30]

But beyond regulation, vérité production was subdued by a new, more broadly based politics of representation. When Allan King claimed in 1983 that his staged confrontation between job-seekers and anonymous management consultants for the CBC vérité special *Who's in Charge* offered subjects "opportunities and resources ... to explore their experience,"[31] many critics were sceptical. Michael Dorland denounced the program for its "sadism" and its "sinister contribution to the television documentary of the future,"[32] while six of its participants (unsuccessfully) went to court, charging King with "invasion of privacy" and "willful infliction of cruelty." These concerns were raised even more vociferously the next decade in response to the *fifth estate*'s "The Trouble with Evan," (1993) a two-hour investigation of a dysfunctional Canadian family which, though better received in some quarters, still reminded other critics of a "hidden surveillance film."[33]

In short, by the 1990s, the future of vérité programming on Canadian television was very much in doubt. To be sure, some critics still associated the genre with public service broadcasting, as evidenced by the popular and critical acclaim that met latter-day productions such as the CBC *National Magazine*'s "Through a Blue Lens" (1999), concerning (once again) Vancouver drug addicts. But the reviews of the 1999 Cinemax vérité production "Men Are from Manhattan, Women from Saskatchewan" shown on the program *Rough Cuts* were perhaps more typical, with the *Globe and Mail*'s John Allemang arguing that "if you've ever thought about documenting your relationship on camera from beginning to end, [programs such as these] should make you see reason."[34] Questions about vérité television, particularly its ability to *represent* and *empower* its subjects, had thus become widespread in Canada by the 1990s. Vérité's legitimacy was at best uncertain in the later years of Canadian public service television.

AN EXAMPLE: *WARRENDALE*

Warrendale is perhaps the most famous portrait of real life ever made for Canadian television. As such, it is a useful case study of the controversies that came to surround vérité programming in its early years in Canada. Warrendale was a centre for disturbed children in Toronto. In 1965 the CBC gave producer Allan King the job of making a film about treatment there. King, who had worked for the CBC for over ten years as a staff member and later as an independent producer, spent a month getting acquainted with the children of the centre and then brought in camera operator William Brayne and sound opertor Russell Heise for two weeks of similar visits. The crew spent a further five weeks shooting the film in and around the centre, eventually editing over 40,000 feet of film into what they hoped would be a hundred-minute TV special.

The resulting film is full of documentary surprises and challenges, even for a contemporary viewer. The opening scene is an unusually lengthy and precise panorama shot of the centre and the Toronto skyline at sunrise, gradually closing in on a car pulling up the driveway of house number 2, the subject of rest of the film. King brings us inside the house, where we follow the social worker as she gets each of her wards out of bed. Nobody speaks much in these scenes, and when they do the sound is generally muffled by background noise due to the absense of "close-miking" technology at the time. Camera work itself is hand-held, shaky, and often out of focus.

Nonetheless these scenes establish the film's story structure and style. *Warrendale* begins and ends as a dawn-to-dusk portrait of a small group of people with little explicit guidance from the filmmakers. Significantly, King and his associates decided early on to forego narration for the film (though the script had been written and supervising producer Patrick Watson hired for the job). Instead, *Warrendale* resorts to a variety of implicit means to situate viewers in the action – focusing, for instance, on metonymic objects that could serve as signposts for the day's locations and events – coffee pots, radios, and dinner tables marking off each room and each ritual of the day. King also follows emblematic personalities whose conflicts (and occasional cooperation) drive the story. Central subjects thus provide narrative structure, allowing the producers to lend a rough chronology and an emotional pace to the story. Walter, the popular young supervisor, appears at regular intervals to save *Warrendale* (as a place and a text) from absolute chaos. Terry, his assistant, is a constant presence instigating the film's conflicts and its "revealing moments." Other characters provide a denouement. Dorothy, the cook, for instance, makes a brief appearance midway through the film only to die in the next scene, setting off the emotional climax of the film.

Beyond imposing a meaningful order on the text, the producers work to *involve* viewers in *Warrendale* and its personalities. True to King's working maxim, the film is part documentary and part soap opera, its story purposely designed as a series of intertwining plots in which viewers can attend to their favourite characters, draw links between scenes, and generally read into the film. Viewers are encouraged to "put in their own stuff," King later observed, adding that "many [at the time] couldn't stand the kids but there were others who found the staff abominable."[35] *Warrendale* thus offered viewers the pleasures of what has since been called a "popular text."[36]

As both information and melodrama, *Warrendale* was regarded by many viewers and critics as an unqualified success. The film won the Palme d'Or at Cannes (along with Antonioni's *Blow Up*) and the top British Academy Award, along with the New York Film Critics' Prize for best picture in 1966. French Director Jean Renoir called King a "great filmmaker," and many Canadian critics were similarly effusive. Martin Knellman, in a 1997 retrospective, pronounced *Warrendale* "the standard against which every documentary about disabled people will have to measured."[37] The film did surprisingly well at the box office, where it sold out many of its North American runs in 1967. In critical and commercial terms, it was perhaps the most successful documentary ever made in Canada.

Yet no film has done more to call into question television's ability to show "life as it really is" in Canada. *Warrendale* was in fact never shown on the CBC and never shown at all on Canadian television until 1997. The corporation, which commissioned the piece, decided it was not in the "best interests of its subjects" (or its viewers, who might be offended by its raw language and emotional violence) and after thirty years sold it back to King, who then took it to TVOntario where it was finally aired. By that time *Warrendale* had become not just a film but a "cause," as critic Peter Goddard put it, symbolizing public service television's inability to honestly deal with Canada at the end of the twentieth century.[38] For critics such as Knellman, *Warrendale* proved once and for all that there was no room in Canadian public service television's safe schedules for programs "getting into social issues in a highly personal and explosive way."[39]

More specifically, *Warrendale* called into question the ability of vérité programming to represent Canada. On the one hand, some critics found *Warrendale's* insights to be indisputable even if they came in the form of emotional catharsis rather than detached anaytical truth. As Stanley Kauffman noted, *Warrendale* was not so much a documentary as an "experience, passionate and compassionate."[40] *Cue* magazine similarly observed that "you are not so much being told about the life of children, you are there."[41] For others, *Warrendale* promised new forms of documentary revelation, a reviewer for the *Sunday Times* noting he could "not imagine anyone coming away from this work unimpressed and unenlightened."[42] "The film reveals to us, more in the way of art than the textbook, something of ourselves," declared the *Financial Times* of London.[43]

For others, however, *Warrendale*'s emotional intimacy fatally undermined its documentary value. For some, the film violated an indexical bond with its viewers, playing with chronology by moving the death of the cook, which had occurred at the start of filming to the middle of the story, to allow for a suitable climax.[44] Some maintained that the intimate style of the film encouraged a type of voyeuristic apathy in its viewers, providing them with an "experience," but little explanation of what was being shown and how they might respond to it. As Greg Quill noted in a retrospective review, "whatever it is that is driving these kids to sudden rage and self-destructive behaviour we never really know – we just have to watch the effects."[45] In this view, *Warrendale* and vérité programs like it provided little sense of what academic critic Bill Nichols in another context called an "an event exceeding representation"[46] – an event requiring any form of follow-up response upon viewing. In short, the *Warrendale* "experience" was seen to be problematic in a public service sense, both as a text and as a call to action.

Perhaps most fundamentally, *Warrendale* seemed to call into question the reality status of Canadian social institutions themselves. For some the film raised the question of the state of Canadian society, the relentlessly physical treatment forced on the children exposing the fine line between love and emotional violence in the country's caretaking insitutions.[47] Others were led to question the existence of Canadian society in the first place, one critic asking, "if this is what has happened to Canadian kids, where are Canadian parents?"[48] *Warrendale* in this view exemplified not just a decline of moral standards amongst youth but a collapse of the normative model of the family. Further, *Warrendale* called into question the existence of an authentic Canadian community, capable of behaving in a spontaneous and natural way under the glare of media publicity. One reviewer noted that "even disturbed children" in Canada seemed to have "taken to pandering to the camera."[49] In these reviews one can discern a deep ambivalence about the film and about Canadian television itself: a celebration of the "authenticity" of the medium, and at the same time a fear that such authenticity was in cultural terms self-defeating. At the very least, many critics felt that televising a Canadian "way of life" exposed its precarious existence and even doomed it as a culture.

To paraphrase Baudrillard, perhaps before his time, Canada in the wake of vérité television seemed to be "disappearing under the weight of its own representation."[50] The form arguably called into question, if only for a moment and if only in some circles, the ability of television to represent the nation to itself – and even more fundamentally, the existence of Canadian social insitutions that might be represented.

DOCUMENTARY ESSAYS

While vérité programs concerned themselves with the most intimate (and often dysfunctional) experiences of Canadian life, long-form documentary essays tended to represent broader, more abstract areas of "national" time and space. These programs offered sweeping interpretations of Canadian history and geography, cumulatively representing the nation from coast to coast and from Confederation to the Centennial. Like vérité programs, they generally did so without recourse to statistical journalistic methods, but here the similarity ends. Long-form documentary essays were designed to document the nation writ large.

The programs were largely creatures of Canada's hundredth anniversary. The CBC kicked off its Centennial project in 1964 with *Camera on Canada,* a series of "visual tone poems" concerning regions across the country. Twelve hour-long "impressions" of Canada's rivers followed in 1965–67 captured by ten cameramen over a two-year period. *Images of Canada*, Vincent Tovell's 1972–74 series of geographical and historical essays, pursued the theme in a more impressionistic manner in the post-Confederation period. The CBC's Centennial television history began in earnest with the *Spirit of '67*, a "major anthology of Canada's first hundred years" produced in 1967.[51] A series of more focused pieces by public affairs producer Cam Graham were then aired, including the 1967 *Hail and Farewell* documenting the final days of John Diefenbaker as leader of the Progressive Conservative Party, the 1968 *The Style Is the Man Himself*, charting Pierre Trudeau's rise to power, and the 1971 *Tenth Decade*, a portrait of the ten-year period leading up to the Centennial. The CBC's director of information programming regarded these programs as "the most important and significant" ever produced by the corporation.[52] None was as costly and ambitious as the 1974 miniseries *The National Dream*, however, a six-hour dramatized account of the building of Canada's national railroad, based on Pierre Berton's book. Other programs such as

Riel were produced (less regularly) in the 1970s, and the tradition continued in the next two decades with specials like CTV's *The Canadians* (1988) and its *Over Canada* (1999), along with the CBC's *Canada: A People's History* (2000).

Documentary specials were eclectic in form and content, but all were seen to contribute to a widespread celebration of Canadian time and space. This involved not just making Canadian history and geography interesting and accessible but first and foremost putting Canada together as a coherent broadcast text. Producers assumed that Canada was dull mostly because it was *distant,* an incomprehensible object to the average Canadian. They thus worked to incorporate Canada's various places and events into a single (sometimes multifaceted) national narrative. This had been a long-term project in Canadian broadcasting. In the 1940s French-language radio producer Robert Bailu had assembled a community in sound by "recording portions of various local events and assembling them on a single disk,"[53] a novel form of "documentary montage" that became a regular feature of his *Les actualites canadiennes* and other programs like it during and after the war. In the 1950s Canadian TV producers developed similar techniques, "blending separate interviews into a syposium on a single theme carried on simultaneously with guests from across the country."[54] Documentary television was seen to be particularly suited to this task. Unlike news, it could facilitate an "extended national conversation." And unlike live broadcasting, it allowed a "variety of people from various corners of the nation" to be compiled into an "astounding and authoritative show."[55]

In short, documentary producers attempted to *imagine* Canada, to tell a national story, as Benedict Anderson has put it, featuring a more or less unified land mass moving along a single trajectory in time.[56] *Camera on Canada*, for instance, represented Canada "in all her rich variety from coast to coast in all four seasons," using a low-flying aircraft to gather a wealth of material which was then edited into a "continuing narrative."[57] It promised an "extraordinary panoramic view ... that few Canadians have the opportunity to see."[58] The *Spirit of '67* dealt with Canadian history by "covering everything of interest Canadians have done in the last 100 years," in a show designed to move along in a "fast and uninterrupted way."[59] Producers of these shows worked to provide Canadians with a continuous and compelling chronology. Given the sheer sweep of the country, many believed that this was a story that only television could tell.

But above and beyond providing a meta-representation of the country at large, documentary specials served a number of more eclectic cultural purposes. Essay programs were seen to animate Canada, bringing it *together,* not just in the text but in the community at large. Many shows were heralded as national events in which Canadians could gather around the TV set in a sort of virtual communion. "I have never felt so Canadian," noted one critic on watching *The National Dream,* "never so part of a national moment of reflection and celebration."[60] Many programs were celebrated as major archival exercises, rescuing images of Canada from the cutting-room floor and thereby laying the foundation for a national memory. In this sense, documentary specials were regarded as something more than mere representation. As many critics noted, they *generated* a national narrative; they *popularized* it; and, in a sense, they *enacted* it, serving as occasions for Canadians to congregate in a moment of self-recognition. Television in this sense was expected to bring the nation into being on a recurring basis.[61] A closer look at one program illustrates the problems the medium encountered in both regards.

AN EXAMPLE: *IMAGES OF CANADA*

Images of Canada was a documentary event conceived as the CBC's most ambitious interpretive essay in the post-Centennial period. Produced by one of the corporation's most consciously intellectual producers, Vincent Tovell, the series consisted of ten hour-long programs concerning Canadian history and geography. Early stories took a chronological and topographical look at Canada. A group of episodes entitled "The Whitecomers" began with a history of New France, moved east to the Maritime Colonies, and west again to Upper Canada, the Prairies, and finally British Columbia. Other sections focused on special topics such as architecture, including a history of the Parliament buildings ("Folly on the Hill"). Later instalments were organized loosely around the reflections of a number of Canadian historians and cultural critics. *Images* took on all these themes in a wide-ranging, eclectic way.[62]

Like many programs in the essay tradition, Tovell's series was special both in terms of the range of its subject matter and the enormous organizational resources the CBC threw into it. Each program cost about $75,000 (more than *Tenth Decade,* less than *The National Dream,* but expensive by the standards of the day), took three to ten months to shoot, and five months to edit. Instalments were then aired as three eighteen-minute acts uninterrupted by commercial breaks. As a CBC press release put it, *Images* was a "Cadillac Information program."[63]

The last instalment aired in 1974 and in many ways typifies the substance and style of the series. *Journey without Arrival* is based on the thoughts and reminiscences of Canadian cultural critic Northrop Frye. Like many of its predecessors, it begins with a Canadian image, a forest in autumn as seen from Frye's train window as he travels across the country. The soundtrack, hard to make out at first, consists of a conductor calling out the stops on CN's Maritime line. We then see Frye himself who, in a voice-over, introduces the theme of the show: "There have been many fables about people who made a long journey only to find that the pot of gold is at the end of the rainbow." But even before the opening credits have rolled, Frye insists, "This is not the Canadian moral." Canadian identity is instead bound up with the "feeling that the end of the rainbow never falls on Canada."

Journey without Arrival's sounds and images steadfastly pursue this theme and are notable for their stylistic range and extraordinary conceptual sweep. After the first commercial, a winter landscape appears, again as seen from Frye's window in the train, while the program's theme music, a modern harp score composed by CBC veteran Louis Applebaum, is gradually superseded by a train whistle and then Frye's reminiscences about his early childhood in Sherbrooke, Quebec. This scene is quickly replaced by an image of a train entering an unidentified farm town in autumn, followed by a quick zoom-in on a photo of Sherbrooke at the time of Frye's childhood, and then a montage of shots of the train and photos of Frye as a child (all of this in less than fifteen seconds of screen time). From off-camera Frye then resumes his story about his move as a boy to Moncton, New Brunswick. His first hometown, he explains, is not a "clear-cut place," being part English and part French, part Protestant and part Catholic. At this point the program has already established its documentary structure, a dizzying array of indexical, iconic, and symbolic sight and sounds, bound together only by the quick evocative cuts of its producer and the irregular presence of a protagonist for whom a structured Canadian identity is problematic. *Journey*'s message and style thus seem designed to call into question conventional modes of documentary realism. Like the rest of the series, it is "part visual essay, part poetry."[64]

Frye and Tovell use this structure to offer a post-colonial "image of Canada" which they admit can never be captured by any medium. "A personal experience of the the Laurentian Thrust is something you have to have. You don't replace it with a book or television," Frye says. Most representations of Canada unwisely seek to impose a categorical order on the landscape. "Flat maps," he continues, "are handy for printing but distort the reality of Canada by portraying the North as an immense looming ghost, framing the country in clear-cut borders where Canada stops at the end of the page." Frye and Tovell's Canada is clearly at odds with this European cartography. Throughout the program its wide endless horizons of nature are juxtaposed with the clear-cut grids of colonial and post-colonial charts, the landscape, according to Frye, resisting all conventional attempts at sense-making. "When you come to Canada, it swallows you," he concludes. "The straits of Belle Isle, the St Lawrence River ... the Great Lakes, they keep going until you've passed the middle of the country, and still you can't say: 'Here we are, we've arrived.'"

Journey without Arrival can be taken as a sustained critique of documentary representation in any form. There is, of course, Frye's insistence on the land and its primacy over colonial logic and myths. And there is Tovell's audiovisual style, with its non-linear, sometimes abstract images, offering plenty of atmosphere but few illustrations of what Frye is actually talking about. *Images* thus seems to forego the indexical authority claimed by NFB documentaries and even journalistic and vérité television reporting at the time.[65] Tovell himself saw the programs as a series of "reflections" (in the contemplative sense) rather than as a conventional travel-logue, drama or documentary.[66]

But for all its flamboyant "anti-realism," *Journey without Arrival* never really gives up on making sense of Canada. Of course its recurring boundless images of Canada can be read as wide "open texts." But more often than not they seem to figure as a sort of "fixed essence" supposedly underlying Europe's artificial grids. It is these recurring images, after all, that allow Frye to make a claim for a Canadian identity logically and chronologically prior to European language and politics. Similarly, the silence of *Journey*'s landscapes can be read as a post-colonial "refusal to represent." But just as plausibly, they can be read as a rather colonial assertion of sense and sensibility concerning the way nature should be appreciated (as the sublime).[67] *Journey* can thus be seen as an attempt to "discover" Canada in the pure, authentic places that only intellectuals can understand. For all its modernist doubts, then, *Images* resurrects Canada as a set of ultimately coherent times and spaces, a sort of "common ground" (the initial title of the series) which viewers can claim as their own.

Judging by contemporary criticism, the program was not an unmitigated success in this regard. Tovell's attempts to "paint a big picture with a broad brush," covering "four centuries by focusing on the traces of dreams in the landscape"[68] left at least some viewers cold and confused. At the program's inception, supervisors had worried about Tovell's "over-intellectualism," recommending a compromise between "bloodlessness and peoplelessness" and a more conventional documentary involving "narrators, actors and graphics."[69] Critics were also ambivalent. Some welcomed *Images* for its sophistication and its ability to "challenge and engage viewers on all levels."[70] Others, such as the *Montreal Gazette*'s L. Ian Macdonald, found the series "dry," noting that "you look at all the wonderful photography and you realize what is missing is people."[71] The *Calgary Herald*'s Bill Musslewhite, in an early review of the series, found Tovell's cross-country, trans-historical approach hard to keep up with, noting that while he had "managed to follow this compendium of history and vegetation through the Maritimes and Upper Canada, he got lost somewhere around Winnipeg."[72] Predictably, many regional critics questioned not just the coherency of the program but its object. "I'm not sure that it is fair to look at the provinces and regions as if they are one geographical, economic and social unit," noted the *Vancouver Sun*'s Lisa Hobbs, further criticizing *Images* for its "misleading impression of a unity through difference."[73] Critics even questioned the show's status as a national event, Jack Nichol admitting that "he dozed off several times" during the proceedings and suggesting that he was probably "not alone."[74]

Journey without Arrival illustrates both the scope and the limitations of Canadian documentary essay programming in its golden years. While many producers and pundits marvelled at the depth and sweep of Tovell's vision, others seemed unsure of its ultimate authenticity and force. *Images* can thus be seen either as a model of television's public service potential, or as proof of its ultimate inability to offer a widely compelling image of Canada, even in the most auspicious of circumstances. In this latter sense, Canada remained a story waiting to be told in the post-Centennial era.

CANADIAN DOCUDRAMAS

Canada's oldest and most critically acclaimed documentary form is neither the vérité investigation nor the interpretive essay but a very different type of "information": the dramatization of real-life events. Television inherited docudramas from radio as a cultural institution. Dramatizations of actual events had been featured in the earliest Canadian radio schedules and became cornerstones of public service broadcasting in the 1930s (see chapter 2). Such programs emerged partly out of necessity, because early technologies did not permit much "real" actuality reporting in the 1920s and '30s. But docudrama was also a widely respected public service form, and was seen to have intrinsic advantages over facts per se. First and foremost in actuality terms, dramatization was able to deal with abstract issues and patterns of events in a way straight documentary reporting could not. "In the space of an hour," the CBC noted, "the Features Department [responsible for many of the early shows] could present the essential aspects of stories such as the war industry or life in the army."[75] In this sense at least, dramatizations were seen to be more "real" than their purely factual counterparts – that is, better able to explore typical as opposed to merely incidental features of any story. The programs were championed in this regard by most of the CBC's educational consultants, with dramatized case studies forming the core of CBC Radio's pedagogical programming and its "in-depth investigations" of Canadian social issues in the 1930s, '40s, and '50s. Similar programs were launched on a smaller scale on Canadian television, where dramatizations were the most common mode of presentation on school broadcasts and regular youth education series such as *Exploring Minds* and *Passe-partout*. Virtually all of these series were prepared with the full cooperation and endorsement of educational groups across the country.[76]

Beyond their virtually unquestioned instructional value, docudramas were also regarded as a popular art. Within documentaries themselves, dramatizations were seen to vary the "aesthetic routine," as producer Gilbert Seldes put it.[77] And they were seen to be formally interesting in their own right, exploring a wider expressive range than either fact or fiction. For critics such as Allan Thomas of the University of British Columbia, docudrama was an "almost perfect type of television documentary" able to illuminate social trends and ideas, with "all the impact of a drama."[78]

Full-fledged criticism of the form only emerged in the 1960s and even then was clearly bound up with concerns about the growing power of television itself. CBC president Alphonse Ouimet, for instance, criticized the drama and documentary program *Quest* for presuming to "probe into "modern attitudes" in a documentary way.[79] Many of his colleagues pointed out such programs were "extremely dangerous ... open to all sorts of abuse and distortion" in the politically charged atmosphere of the 1960s.[80] In the wake of the 1958–59 CBC producer's strike and the debates it engendered over televisual authority, docudramas became particularly controversial as *commentary*. It was at this time that dramatized specials such as the CBC's *Open Grave* (1963) began to be accompanied by factual disclaimers, a peculiar precedent given the corporation's earlier policy of not identifying reenactments nor frequently even the names of actors in closing credits. By the early 1960s then, docudramas came to be seen by critics and advocates alike as a forum for journalistic activism, a handy vehicle for public affairs producers to interpret and pass judgment on contemporary social life.

Further controversies in the 1970s and '80s must also be understood in the context of increasing anxieties about television and specifically television journalism. Programs such as Denis Arcand's *Duplessis* (1980) on the French network were welcomed by some critics but disparaged by others as historical debunking. The CBC's out-of-court settlement with Peter Lougheed following a *For the Record* dramatization in 1977 of the Alberta Tar Sands deal was not necessarily a decisive defeat for the genre as a television form, as some academic critics feared[81] – indeed *For the Record*'s producers claimed they were making mere "topical dramas" rather than strict historical reconstructions per se. But it did further call into quesion the practice of using actors to portray active public figures. More fundamentally, it cast doubt on the rights of journalists to interpret Canada's past and its living history.

But if docudrama has been at the centre of a number of debates concerning television and cultural authority, we should bear in mind that these debates have almost always been explicitly *political* rather than *epistemological* in nature. That is, they have centred on the rights of journalists to produce and interpret knowledge rather than on the status of knowledge itself. While the genre was championed by academic critics for its supposedly subversive qualities – specifically, its "refusal" of narrative closure and objectivity[82] – examples of such documentary "progressive realism" were (and are) few and far between on Canadian television. Its best known docudramas, including the CBC's *Canada's Sweetheart* (1985), *King Chronicles* (1988), *The Boys of St Vincent* (1991), and *The Valour and the Horror* (1992), have resorted to reenactments to fill in a gap in the historical archives. But none has used the form to interrogate documentary "truth" in a substantive or sustained way – certainly none called into question the naturalness of its *own* point of view on these grounds. Generally speaking, then, these programs should be read as historical *reconstructions*, working within well-worn traditions of documentary realism in Canada.

All of this is worth keeping in mind as docudrama is perhaps Canada's most misunderstood documentary form: hardly a foreign or corrupt genre as some critics have charged, epitomizing instead Canadian public service traditions of pedagogy and social realism; and hardly a poster program for postmodern or progressive realism, as some supporters have claimed, calling into question not so much the philosophical status of documentary knowledge as the rights of certain groups to define it. At first glance, then, docudramas have hardly been alien or subversive in Canada. Yet no documentary form has done as much to call into question the right, if not the ability, of Canadian television to represent the nation to itself.

AN EXAMPLE: *THE VALOUR AND THE HORROR*

Perhaps the most popular and provocative example of Canadian docudrama television has been *The Valour and the Horror*, a three-part series made for the CBC, tackling various aspects of Canada's role in World War II. The program itself was hugely ambitious, costing $2.8 million in total and taking three years to make. Its producers, Gala Films of Montreal, drew on archive footage from the U.S., Britain, Germany, and Japan, with the editorial assistance of the CBC and the National Film Board. *Valour* ended up winning possibly the largest documentary audience in Canadian history, with well over four million English-language viewers and 350,000 French-language viewers tuning in for all three episodes (averaging over 20 per cent of the Canadian audience).[83]

At the same time, controversy surrounding the program was fierce and immediate. Internal and external investigations were launched in short order by the Canadian Senate's Committee on Veteran Affairs, the CRTC, the CBC's Office of the President and Ombudsman, and finally a number of Canadian courts. The veterans' lawsuit charging the program with historical inaccuracy was dismissed by the Supreme Court in 1996, and the Senate's hearing was perhaps a foregone conclusion (it resulted in the program's being roundly censured). The CBC's own Ombudsman's report dealt the program, and dramatized information in general, a particularly serious blow. In his final report Ombudsman William Morgan concluded that *Valour*'s "most significant areas of difficulty" involved dramatization techniques per se rather than any particular usage of them, techniques which, he insisted, lent the "appearance of reality to hypothesis," potentially confusing audiences over the nature of the information being received.[84] Morgan argued that there was actually no precedent for dramatization of this type on Canadian public television. He dismissed earlier programs in the tradition as either "full-blown dramas," or else probable violations of policy that should not have been allowed on air in the first place.[85] In short, Morgan denied docudrama's past at the CBC, and while he did not rule out its future as a separate or contained program type (albeit with markers and disclaimers attached), he did seem to question for the first time its overall status as a legitimate public service form.

The subject of most of Morgan's remarks, and the focus of most of the criticism directed at the series, was the second instalment, "Death by Moonlight." This program, more than any other, was seen to have mixed fact and fiction, confusing viewers with unidentified recreations, inexact quotes, and an improper use of actors and dramatic devices. The program, which concerns the bombing of Germany by Allied bombers in the closing stages of World War II, is worth examining in some detail to understand the conventions and controversies that have come to surround this documentary form in recent years.

"Death by Moonlight" uses many reenactments and makes strong claims for them as documentary evidence. "This is a true story," announces producer and narrator Terrence McKenna at the start of the show. "In some case actors speak words of soldiers and nurses. There is no fiction." The program proceeds to offer a rapid-fire collage of sounds and images to make its case against the Allied bombing. Scene one shows "traces" of the raids themselves, as seen in the ruins of the Yorkshire airbases; scene two introduces surviving airmen who provide oral testimony concerning what it was like to be part of the campaign; subsequent scenes offer period photos, recorded songs, and finally full-fledged reenactments as "documents" of the events concerned.

For all its stylistic range, however, it is hard to see how fact and fiction are confused in "Death by Moonlight." To be sure, a variety of sounds and images are presented as building blocks in the producer's case against the bombing. Yet each stage of the argument seems to be marked off as as a distinct type of documentary fact. The program's first reenactment of a soldier's night out before a mission, for instance, is carefully differentiated stylistically from the actuality segments that preceded it. Camera work is not handheld and uninterrupted as is typical of the show's actuality shots. Instead, images are fixed and clearly edited into a series of shots, mastershots, and precisely controlled close-ups. In this sense the scenes offer a typical fictional lexicon with which viewers are presumably familiar. Similarly, these scenes dispense with conventional documentary framing, with subjects precisely captured rather than randomly "found" in their images. Finally, the reenactments forego a documentary-type soundtrack, offering a limited number of dramatically important voices and sounds – the singing of actors, the reading of a soliloquy, for example – to provide a clear narrative thrust. Overall, then, the scenes are distinguished by the precision of their sounds and images and by the careful placing of the viewer in relation to the action on the screen.[86]

Fictional styles similarly mark out the most controversial reenactments of the series, involving Bomber Command Chief Arthur Harris. Here, in contrast to the show's "actual" subjects, an actor is lit by high-key studio lighting against an iconic black backdrop, speaking directly to viewers in soliloquy fashion with no background noise other than the dramatic rhythmic clicking of his Zippo lighter. Again, this scene is distinguished by the controlled economy of its sounds and images.

Not only are fact and fiction clearly (if implicitly) marked in "Death by Moonlight" but the program often relies on our ability to distinguish them to follow its main argument. Wartime newsreels are generally offered not as straightforward documentary reportage but as *disinformation*, with the producers counting on our familiarity (and latent distrust) of propaganda and public relations to put the material in proper perspective. Without a reasonably sophisticated "decoding" of this material, the program would be quite incoherent as an argument. In this way "Death by Moonlight" builds its case not by blurring levels of documentary evidence but by careful and rather conventional *juxtaposition* of narrative assertion, actuality footage, and dramatized sounds, images, and graphics. In style if not substance, "Death by Moonlight" is true to the well-established traditions of Canadian public service documentary progamming.

Neither, finally, is there much *contextual* evidence to suggest a confusion of fact and fiction in the program, or even a strategic use of reenactments to manipulate viewers. A CBC panel of two hundred viewers ranked the commentary of the veterans as the program's most compelling piece of evidence, followed by film footage, voice-over commentary, and, in last place, dramatic portrayals.[87] Charges of deliberate obfuscation of fact and fiction in the program thus seem somewhat specious. Charges of program imbalance are more plausible, though similarly difficult to sustain. While the program certainly organizes its material around a revisionist reading of World War II, it is worth remembering that more controversial interpretations of the Allied bombing campaigns have for years been given pride of place on the public network, including Richard Nielsen's two-part investigation (1965) of the bombing of Dresden for the *Public Eye* series, and his 1998 *Remembering Canadians at War*, a feature program generally viewed as a sort of television documentary rebuttal to *The Valour and the Horror*.[88]

Why then was *The Valour and the Horror* so controversial? What made the program the touchstone it became for the criticism of investigative journalism and public service broadcasting in Canada? The reasons are perhaps both textual and contextual in nature. David Taras is right to argue that *any* program taking on a powerful lobby group such as the veterans was a likely target during the Mulroney years, particularly under the tenure of a conservative activist CBC board of directors.[89] But *The Valour and the Horror* may have been vulnerable not just because of what it said, and when it said it: also at issue was the program's form of presentation. Clearly, docudrama, like no other documentary style, bought to the fore the issue of journalistic intervention – which, as Taras and others have noted, was becoming a matter of concern to a number of cultural authorities in the early 1990s. For *The Valour and the Horror*, producer-journalists *generated* an archive, *reconstructed* their own documentary evidence in the form of reenactments, and frequently *reinterpreted* and *undermined* existing historical data through various forms of deconstructive montage. Producers Brian and Terrence McKenna sought a good degree of footage beyond the usual stock sources and used diaries, letters, and latter-day interviews to generate scripts for their actors. They also entered into what they called a "partnership" with library archivists, using new indexing and sampling systems to produce a unique visual record.[90] Docudrama in the hands of the McKennas thus emerged as an alternative historical "discourse" with its own authorities of delimitation and its own relationships to other conceptual fields. Brian McKenna implicitly made just such a claim when he criticized Canadian historians for their lack of courage "in not drawing the conclusions" that he "found in their own evidence."[91]

Groundbreaking or not, the "truth" of "Death by Moonlight" was clearly the result of massive and transparent journalistic intervention at every stage of the program's production. This was an obviously assembled piece of work, aired at a time when journalistic knowledge and intervention were possibly more controversial than at any other time in Canadian history. It was thus neither the form nor the content of the program – neither the text nor its context – but a peculiar conjuncture of each at a particular moment in time which undermined the credibility of docudrama as a legitimate form of public expression in the 1990s and perhaps the years beyond.

DOCUMENTARY JOURNALISM

For all the attention (critical or otherwise) garnered by vérité programs, long-form essays, and docudramas, the most important genre of Canadian documentary television in terms of sheer output and stylistic influence has always been the investigative journalistic report. Journalistic documentaries have been a mainstay of Canadian television since its first days on the air, when programs such as

Tabloid, Newsmagazine, and *Point de mire* featured fast-breaking documentary reports that adhered to news program standards of style and objectivity (see chapter 3). However, the wholesale transformation of television documentary into a journalistic form – with other forms of documentary surviving as complementary but subsidiary types – was largely the result of three latter-day developments: the integration of news and public affairs departments, the development of more precise guidelines concerning information programming, and finally, the stricter day-to-day supervision of documentary production in the late 1960s and the decades that followed.

The integration of news and public affairs departments at the CBC began in earnest following the cancellation of *This Hour Has Seven Days* and the organizational shake-up that followed.[92] The CBC moved to coordinate production in the news and public affairs areas along the lines of operations at the CTV network where programs such as *W5* had always been one-department (i.e., news) productions. At the public network, hybrid news and public affairs programs were introduced on a grand scale in 1966 when programs such as *This Week* began to be planned and produced by both departments in a shared studio space.[93] In 1969, after years of competition, operations were formally merged into a single news and current affairs unit.

In other ways as well the corporation moved to establish a unified information service based on journalistic modes of actuality. In the late 1960s and '70s it introduced new regulations concerning documentary ethics and objectivity in a series of increasingly lengthy and detailed journalistic policy guides. Areas as diverse as accuracy (the "conformity of information to reality"), integrity (the "avoidance of personal bias"), and balance (the "equitable reflection of facts and significant points of view") were dealt with in increasingly legalistic detail.[94] Practices associated with other types of documentary television, such as the "use of clandestine methods" in vérité reporting, and the mixture of actuality and dramatization in docudramas, were also regulated according to journalistic principles of fairness and facticity.

The repercussions for documentary programming at the CBC were radical if not immediate. For instance, new rules concerning objectivity led to internal investigations of programs such as *Air of Death* (1967), an Agriculture and Resources department production concerning pollution problems in Eastern Canada. *Adieu alouette*

(1973), an NFB feature, was reprimanded for its "editorial comments" on the FLQ Crisis[95] (the CBC, according to one internal memo, hoped to stop the "politicization of NFB productions" from spreading to its network[96]). Hosts were also vetted for their "partisanship," among them Radio Canada veteran René Lévesque who was barred from presenting *Tuesday Night* documentaries because of his identification with Quebec nationalism. At the same time, more precise restrictions regarding the mixing of actuality and fiction forms led to the pulling of satire segments from information shows such as *Up Canada,* and the extensive re-editing of others, including another story about Quebec for *Tuesday Night,* in which the use of sound loops of explosions and gunfire over a reading of an FLQ manifesto was deemed to be excessively "sensationalistic." Overall, new rules were meant to ensure a "more disciplined use of language and production techniques, including visuals."[97]

The corporation also developed more effective procedures for enforcing these journalistic standards on a day-to-day basis. Documentary supervision was, of course, nothing new at the CBC, where news officials had tried to promote "fair" documentary programming from the start. The first assistant director of programs, for instance, had expressed concerns about the "accuracy, reliability and balance" of documentaries in 1954, noting that such programs were just as "sensitive as news broadcasts and rather harder to handle by ready-made regulations."[98] After the 1958–59 producers' strike, CBC headquarters in Ottawa further regulated the genre by increasing control over production departments, culminating eventually in the dismantling of autonomous program units – most notably, the *Document* series in the wake of the *Seven Days* controversy. Producers also began to work under increasing commercial pressures, as a more aggressive CBC sales department demanded detailed program plans to help sell documentary series to advertisers.[99]

For all these reasons, documentary programming was largely colonized by journalism in its middle years. By 1973 programs were being routinely monitored and classified for their controversiality (ranging from *This Land* at the low end of the scale to *Weekend* at the high end).[100] Shows were also subject to an increasingly elaborate range of reviews and previews to "monitor editorial direction, content balance and policy implementation."[101] During the *fifth estate*'s 1977 season, initial story ideas had to be approved by executive producers, senior producers, and unit managers to ensure a "common set of objectives" before being developed as full treatments – story proposals of fifteen to twenty pages. These drafts were presented to the executive producer for amendment, and then again for a final evaluation concerning length, cost, and "fit within the overall content of the series." Once in the field, producers were expected to submit to senior producers of the show transcripts and films of all interviews conducted on location. Managers would then examine the rough cuts for "editorial content, fairness, legal questions and production qualities," after which new versions would be reviewed and probably revised several times before airtime. Programs that made it this far would then be screened at least once more by the CBC's director of news and current affairs and associated area heads, and cassettes would be kept on hand for year-end evaluations. The whole process could take months and sometimes years but was considered to be "worthwhile" for all concerned.[102] The end result was more journalistic standardization at the corporation.

Of course news and current affairs dominance was never absolute at the CBC. Journalistic supervision was hardly foolproof. As the CBC's head of current affairs noted, the pre-screening of all documentary programs was actually "just about impossible," given the volume of work being turned out.[103] Daily current affairs shows were particularly hard to monitor, given the pace of production schedules. Even a long-planned and much anticipated 1974 *fifth estate* story concerning the CIA and Canadian intelligence, which CBC officials feared might be in violation of Canada's Official Secrets Act, was only screened by the director of information programming one hour before airtime rather than "several weeks before as it should have been."[104]

Further, a good many series and features explicitly rejected journalistic formats, both inside and outside the news and current affairs unit. Regular programs such as *Man Alive*, for instance, produced "viewer-friendly" point of view documentaries throughout the 1970s, '80s and '90s, while *The Nature of Things* focused on "in-depth stories not seen on the news."[105] These programs may not have been radical or "counter-hegemonic," but they offered something more than traditional current affairs journalism, focusing as they did on long-term issues, and produced as they were by specialized semi-permanent production units often in cooperation with non-professional program consultants. Non-journalistic aesthetics survived in public affairs programming as well, with producers such as Martyn Burke offering occasional "poetic stories," including a February 1971 item for *Newsmagazine* in which educator Ivan Illich was shot entirely in silhouette, his image occasionally dissolving into the pyramids near his home to "show his closeness to the Mexican landscape."[106] This was not the sort of approach favoured in journalistic stylebooks.

But if non-journalistic documentary was never entirely eliminated, the CBC had at least *begun* to erect a "single cohesive information service"[107] in which journalistic conventions of style and substance became the norm and all others types the exceptions. The new rules were certainly reflected in network schedules of the mid-1970s. *Fifth estate*, for instance, was designed to be "investigative and provocative" without being "reckless," always adhering to journalistic principles of fairness, balance, and clarity of exposition.[108] *Marketplace* was similarly founded on a "commitment to "solid journalistic standards" combined with a "fervent belief in the cause of consumerism."[109] Even self-styled point of view programs like *Ombudsman* (billed as a spirited "fight for the underdog") promised to respect "established notions of fairness and justice in information programming."[110]

The journalistic tradition had become established at other networks as well. At Radio Canada where notions of balance and linear expositions were somewhat more flexible, journalistic programs like *Le 60*, *Telemagazine*, and later *Le Point* and *L'Enjeux* were still promoted as the network's "most outstanding documentary features" and as models of its "consistent standards and levels of quality."[111] Similarly, CTV's prestige information program *W5* promised to provide "in-depth journalistic reports albeit with a confrontational edge" which could always be counted on for "uniform standards of journalistic excellence."[112]

Clearly, then, Canadian television networks had begun to produce more and more documentary programs whose reliability was seen to derive from abstract principles of fairness and balance rather than the vision or point of view of any individual producers. In this sense at least, documentary programming had become standardized along journalistic lines in Canada. It was thus the journalistic report, and the national news and current affairs apparatus that supported it, that in the 1970s and '80s carried the main burden of documenting the nation.

CHALLENGES TO DOCUMENTARY
JOURNALISM

Challenges to documentary journalism came from two main sources: from Canada's regions and localities, and from its proliferating multicultural communities. Pressures for more regional representation in information programming had begun in earnest with the tabling of the 1957 Fowler Report which called for representation of areas outside Ontario in all areas of television. Early attempts at local documentary programming included *Pacific 13* (1957), a regionally focused magazine program produced out of Vancouver and, in the next decade, *Camera West*. In the long-form documentary area, the corporation experimented with simultaneous documentary broadcasts on the French and English networks; *Premier Plan* and *Explorations*, for instance, offered a pioneering 1959 co-production concerning the conquest of Quebec.[113] All these programs were designed to introduce Canadian regions to each other's cultures – as represented and mediated on the national documentary network.

But regional documentary programming became more of a priority at the CBC in the early 1970s, when provincial public broadcasting services were established across Canada, and the CRTC began to call for "greater regional participation in network programming."[114] The CBC's response to these pressures was almost immediate, if fairly predictable. A limited reorganization of all areas of programming had already taken place at the English network in 1968, and a similar plan was put into effect for documentary programming, with some current affairs production facilities moved to larger regional centres in 1972 and 1973.[115] The thrust of the corporation's regionalization plan, however, involved improving "the routine workings" of its national, mostly Ottawa-based departments by establishing content quotas and a regional program ombudsman. Overall, the network promised the regions a "fair chance at [national] documentary slots."[116] Further and somewhat paradoxically, the corporation tried to eliminate old local program exchanges, which were seen to favour generic general-interest shows, replacing them with a national system ensuring an "appropriate degree of local orientation" in documentary features.[117]

Regional producers and communities demanded something more than content quotas and better production facilities, however. Regional producer associations objected to centrally mandated "regionalism" per se – that is, to the network's insistence that regional units only deal with "regional stories" as defined by Central Canada. The Alberta producers association insisted that a 1974 feature by CBC Edmonton on sex shops was "not by nature not local,"[118] while Ottawa producers noted that a story about fugitive activist Jerry Rubin might not have concerned a local personality but certainly was of "local interest."[119] For these producers, the network's system of licensed pluralism in the early 1970s became increasingly intolerable.

Local communities (or at least their media representatives) also took exception to the network's regional representation system. The *Halifax Chronicle-Herald* (no friend of the public network at the best of times) objected to the network's "patronizing tone" and to its "miserable lampoons" of outlying areas.[120] Others criticized the national network's "soft-focus sentimental image" of local communities and questioned the use of such "visual monotony."[121] Critics also questioned the *benefits* of documentary programs for the regions themselves. In Welland, Ontario, for instance – the subject of a CBC *Tuesday Night* investigation of "drug use in small towns" – the town council wondered how it would overcome the "adverse publicity" resulting from the show and questioned what was to be "gained for the community" from such a national exposé.[122] Other disgruntled locales such as Inuvik and Orillia criticized the *one-way communication* of the documentary network, demanding that producers appear before their communities to answer for their programs, a request almost invariably denied, with producers such as Larry Gosnell of *Tuesday Night* insisting there was "nothing to be gained from such meetings ... [which] would almost certainly lead to confrontation."[123]

By the 1970s many producers and viewers were clearly beginning to question the whole logic of the documentary network: its regional classification systems, its standardized aesthetic, its supervisory protocols, and its relentlessly unilinear mode of communication. In this sense at least, documentary television seemed increasingly unable to represent the nation in all its regional diversity. As TV current affairs head John Kerr admitted, the network was structurally incapable of dealing with regional demands, its reforms simply giving rise to expectations "beyond our ability or hours to accomodate them."[124] Other officials despaired of a lasting regional solution because there was no longer any consensus concerning "what an accurate regional representation might be."[125]

Further and even more hopeless challenges to the documentary network came from Canada's multicultural communities, whose demands called into question not just particular allocations of resources or modes of representation but the basic working principles of the information network. In the 1970s in particular many community critics demanded more adequate network representation, but also direct access to production facilities, and thus the elimination of all forms of mediation from the process of documentation. Documentary professionalism itself came under fire.

Pressures for *access* per se arose in the context of changes in Canadian film and television at the time. The emergence of a number of community self-representation projects on the new cable channels,[126] along with a series of National Film Board community "self-documentation" projects,[127] were factors. So were policy hearings at the CRTC, where complaints from a number of unions and senior citizen and multicultural and religious organizations were heard in 1973. Virtually none of these groups believed their concerns could be adequately accomodated within television's existing network system.

The corporation also had to answer direct criticisms from a number of "ethnic" communities who felt that they had been not only ill-served but almost entirely *excluded* from the information network. The complaints of native groups were particularly vexing in this regard. By the CBC's own account, until the early 1960s "odd single programs" had been done on natives but there had "never been a solid [documentary] series."[128] More programs were introduced in the years that followed, but according to Harold Cardinal, president of the Indian Association of Alberta, even in the early 1970s "Indian people [were] rarely allowed to express in their own words and their own manner what it is they felt, without the intrusion of a narrator."[129] While the corporation expressed sympathy with the complaints, demands that natives be *consulted* concerning the content and style of their depiction were generally rejected on the grounds that voices and images were not the property of individuals or communities who "consented to be filmed."[130]

How then to address these escalating demands for representation and self-documentation in documentary television's third decade? Officials considered a number of measures. Many programs established audience consultation systems, like those maintained for years by programs such as *Man Alive*. Magazine shows such as

Take 30 and *Tuesday Night* introduced "theme shows" focusing on issues of concern to particular communities. The network itself tentatively embraced public access programming under controlled conditions, trying out a number of formats in this area. In 1974 the corporation launched CBC *Access*, in which communities produced films about themselves under the supervision of veteran Ross McLean. *Ombudsman* offered CBC-produced films dealing with viewer complaints. Later in the decade limited access features were introduced on regular series such as *Take 30*, and in the 1980s the CBC considered allowing groups such as the newly formed Canadian Independent Film Caucus direct access to its ill-fated CBC-2 cultural channel.[131]

But public service broadcasters had doubts from the start about even these limited forms of "self-documentation." Current affairs head John Kerr believed that access programming was often "synonymous with partisan programming" and fundamentally at odds with CBC editorial traditions.[132] Knowlton Nash viewed it as an unsustainable form, almost certainly lacking in "audience appeal."[133] Peter Herrndorff regarded the genre as a "danger area" that would have to remain under CBC control guided by "sound journalistic judgment."[134] Indeed, "public access" at the CBC seems to have been largely designed to head off more radical community challenges: Herrndorff maintained that the CBC should act on the matter "before public pressure narrows our range of choices."

In short, the corporation did everything it could to accomodate demands for diverse representation within the confines of the national information network. Programmers attempted to *circumvent* difference by going over the heads of "interest groups" and offering programs that related to generic "human interests" rather than diverse communities as such,[135] clearly hoping to speak to audiences as individual viewers rather than collective producers. Further, they worked to *marginalize* difference, by defining and addressing it only in relation to a core "national identity," insisting, as Peter Herrndorff did, that access programs deal with stories "that are common and important to all Canadians."[136] Finally, they attempted to *administer* difference by organizing audiences into fixed interest categories within the confines of the network schedule – offering limited program slots, for instance, to a select number of claimants on a "proportional" basis.

But for all this bureaucratic manœuvring, and the derisive dismissal of "self-documentation" as a workable public service model, access demands did raise what for programmers were larger issues concerning the need for more compelling modes of televisual representation. Documentary programs in particular were seen to lack relevancy and zip, and to have become increasingly abstract and distant from viewers' lives. The network somehow had to produce shows that would "speak to viewers right where they are."[137] This need for proximity became particularly pressing in the late 1970s and early '80s, as the CBC began to confront the spectre of the specialty channel – specifically, information television that could address viewers as special interests in a way the national network never could. As documentary television in Canada entered its fourth decade, then, it was widely seen to be grasping for new forms of representation that could "build a community of interest with the audience."[138]

AN EXAMPLE: *THE JOURNAL*

It was in the context of these challenges that the CBC launched *The Journal* in 1982. Faced with pressures from localities, from regulators, and from would-be alternative telecasters, coupled with a steady decline in its audience share, the corporation undertook what it called the "boldest programming move in its history."[139] In any circumstances *The Journal* would have been something more than a run-of-the-mill current affairs show. After all, it was replacing the longest-running newscast in North American history with a thirty-six minute interview and documentary program following the news, hosted by two women – with a start-up budget of $7 to 10 million. The program was seen to be a gamble, indeed a survival test for public service television in a new broadcasting environment. If the new show failed, noted Mark Daigneault, head of news and current affairs, it would be "worse than a body blow for the corporation, more like a technical knockout."[140] Hyperbole aside, *The Journal* was in the eyes of many public service television's last chance to represent the nation to what was left of its national audience.

In many respects *The Journal* was the culmination of a long line of public affairs programs designed to accessibly represent Canadian life. The roots of the show can be traced back to *Tabloid* and *Newsmagazine*'s documentary-style features on issues behind the news, and to what Ross McLean called his "pocket documentaries" for CBC *Close-Up* in the 1950s (see chapter 3). The program was also a natural outgrowth of the recently integrated news and current affairs operations at the CBC, which at least since the mid-1960s had included plans for some sort of current affairs program within the national newscast. But more fundamentally, *The Journal* was simply the continuation of a long-term public service project to eliminate television's distance from Canadian life – to get information from subjects and bring it to viewers in more direct and immediate ways. "Getting closer to Canada" had always been a goal of programs such as *Take 30*, which in the 1960s had conceived a strategy to "get on the phone and in a couple of hours come up with an half-hour documentary by remote control."[141] Daytime current affairs television had thus worked to create a virtual national space like the one executive producer Mark Starowicz and his colleagues were now talking about, what they referred to as an "electronic village pump" where ideas could be pooled and a constant interregional dialogue maintained. These producers in turn were guided by phone-in radio programs which, from the early 1960s, had used switching systems to foster a sense of two-way communication with their audiences, a rudimentary "interactive" method later adopted by network radio shows such as *As It Happens*.

Like its predecessors, *The Journal* essentially relied on new technologies to bridge television's distance in time and space from Canadian affairs. Producers tried to make their programs more immediate by using new video production and processing facilities to produce over 250 documentaries a year – the largest documentary output in North America, yielding what producers called an "ongoing record of Canadian life."[142] Documentary reports were also designed to *look* closer in time to the events they were about, using new types of videotape with a "live feel" rather than the softer, more old-fashioned images of film. At the same time producers worked to bridge the *space* gap by more effectively "covering the country," notifying all regional affiliates by telex of upcoming assignments in which they might participate, while themselves covering more regional events with portable electronic cameras and satellite up-links. According to Mark Starowicz, *The Journal*'s new information technologies would allow a fisherman to be interviewed "right on his boat live via satellite" and thereby "break down the dominance of the urban" in public service television.[143] Sounds and images of the margins were to be reconfigured within the text itself: "squeezooms" would reduce pictures and combine them with others from across the country, while "double enders" would give the illusion of a face-to-face dialogue between the host and Canada's outlying communities. With these new *technologies of proximity, The Journal* worked to integrate Canada's multiplying margins into a new, more inclusive national media space.

The 1985 *Journal* documentary "The Forgotten Pioneers" is an example of such a project and the challenges it faced in the later years of public service television. The report, which was re-broadcast in 1989, concerned a group of native Inuit from Quebec who had been moved to the northernmost reaches of Canada to support its claims to Arctic sovereignty during the Cold War. Explained host Valerie Pringle in 1989, "Five years ago when we first aired this story, everyone agreed on the basic facts. As we'll see this evening, that is no longer the case."

The documentary report itself begins with a silent image of an iceberg surrounded by swirling misty water. Reporter Bruce Garvey immediately situates the picture, "through the polar iceberg of the High Arctic, 1,100 kilometres north of the Arctic Circle. The ice never totally melts here," he tell us, "even when a summer mist hangs over Canada's most notherly community." We are shown a hill-top shot of a small image of Grise Fjord, a "setting for a story you won't find in the history books."

The inhabitants of the town, Garvey says, "still use the traditional ways, and life here would appear to have evolved that way." Images appear of men and women cleaning fish and stretching sealskins. "But it didn't," notes Garvey, now directly addressing the audience. "These people are not natural inhabitants. They're transplanted here and in fact they're a long way from home." The on-the-scene reporter then introduces the main topic of the program: "This is the story of an amazing little group of transplanted pioneers that almost nobody outside the North has heard about."

Still in Grise Fjord, he proceeds to explain how the story began, tracing its origins to Canada's struggles with Denmark, Norway, and finally the u.s. "This was the backdrop to the annual voyage of the medical and supply ship C.D. Howe, which in 1953 carried six Inuit families from Port Harrison, Quebec, for resettlement." Archive footage of the ship is shown, followed by a map of Canada with Port Harrison at its centre, showing the slow progress of the ship that year to the edge of the map – Resolute Bay, where the first three families were dropped off, and then Grise Fjord on Ellesmere Island.

A number of experts reflect on the reasons behind the move. Inuit resettlement was "essentially an advancement of sovereignty," explains a senior government advisor for the project. "The government put us here and just forgot about us. I think we didn't count at all," responds Larry Oudooluk, who was moved to Ellesmere as a child. "My family remember how when we came here there was nothing," he explains in a voice-over of a collage of images of Grise Fjord today, beginning with shots of a wave crashing on an icefloe, a lone bird gliding in the sky, and finally the stark mountains and glaciers towering above the town at daybreak.

Further testimony follows, from a mother who was separated from her daughter for three years during the move, and a younger woman, now a native activist in Ottawa, who remembers having to wear a dog tag marked "E" for "Eskimo." Inhabitants of Resolute Bay similarly remember how they were "just dumped" and subsequently mistreated by Canadian officials. "From all these children of '53," concludes Garvey, "you now hear the same demands: for compensation, but more, for recognition."

"The government owes us," says Mary Flaheety of Grise Fjord, "because we were fooled by what they promised."

"Why do you think this is being hushed up in the South?" asks Garvey.

"Shame," answers Flaheety.

"Have they deliberately swept it under the rug?"

"I think they used us, definitely," replies Flaheety, concluding the segment.

The scene switches to Parliament Hill, with Garvey noting in a voice-over that the "politicians of the '50s are gone now, and their successors have very different attitudes to native peoples and grievances." He then is shown in a brief interview with then-minister of Indian and Northern Affairs, David Crombie, who explains that he is "concerned about the case but not sure of the answer of how to resolve it."

"Eloquently concerned but not quite sure of the answer," sums up the reporter, who concludes, directly addressing the camera back in Resolute Bay: "For the Inuit who pioneered [this land] and struggled to put down those fragile roots of settlement and sovereignty, the recognition of history has yet to catch up."

"But the story is far from over," adds host Valerie Pringle in an update from the *Journal* studio, "and it may be heading towards a major collision between government and Inuit." The 1989 broadcast closes with an interview with Dr Richard van Loon, then senior deputy assistant of Indian and Northern Affairs, and John Amogoalik, president of the Inuit Tapirisat of Canada, each explaining their positions concerning compensation, in opposition to the Conservative government of the day.

"Forgotten Pioneers" is typical of the style and format of many *Journal* reports, based on a rather straight journalistic narrative that begins with a situation (natives in homeland) a complication (resettlement), and a provisional resolution (recognition and compensation for the Inuit). The use of sounds and images is for the most part efficient rather than evocative, with people and places serving as metonyms to advance the story and its argument. Editing is functional and concise with no interview lasting longer than eighteen seconds.

Also like most other *Journal* reports, the story makes elaborate efforts to accomodate Canadian cultural difference. The program repeatedly, if implicitly, promises to restore the Inuit to a central position in Canadian society, visually moving them from the edges of the map (where they have been shunted by an accident of history) to the centre, which for *The Journal*'s purposes this night is Port Harrison, Quebec. The program then provides the Inuit with a new position from which they can engage in dialogue and hope to gain recognition, providing not just a (more or less authentic) site of representation but a space for the recovery of community – a space where the Inuit can regain their voice, their identity, their history and their rightful "place on the map." *The Journal* thus presents itself as a virtual *public sphere* that allows (but always mediates) the Inuit's dialogue with the outside world. Perhaps significantly, the Indian and Northern Affairs minister and the Inuit Tapirisat spokesperson are shown in separate graphics, framed by the *Journal* logo throughout the discussion period, though as we learn at the end of the show they are actually sitting side by side for a debate taped earlier in Ottawa. In short, *The Journal* offers what Steven Jones has, in another context, called a "furious simulation" of a community[144] – a space that claims to faithfully record difference and allow for interaction as the first step towards the recovery of a stable identity. The program thus presents itself not just as a useful accessory but a *condition of possibility* for cultural difference.

Yet at the same time *The Journal* acknowledges its own limits in representing and recovering Port Harrison. As Pringle notes in the update, many Inuit are "no longer preoccupied with the dispute," and others disagree on the nature of a just settlement, a claim that seems at odds with the program's depiction of a united and rooted community whose views can be incorporated into conventional journalistic categories within the space of a very occasional thirty-minute national airing. Further, the program's effort to give voice to a forgotten people is undermined by its own rigid expositional structure in which images and testimony are used solely to advance a central proposition: that the Inuit have been used as pawns in the sovereignty game. Inuit images are brief and Inuit testimony is purely functional, always serving to advance an argument permitting little elaboration or digression. The program itself seems to acknowledge the inadequacy of such representation by offering itself first as a story behind the news event and then as an interview behind the story, in an attempt to get at "what the Inuit really want." In all these respects, as one reviewer of the time put it, *The Journal* appears as a representation of Canada and its various communities, searching for but "never quite achieving substance."[145] Another concluded when the program went off the air in 1991 that *The Journal's* national reports were "always intriguing" but "more postcards than documentaries."[146] Whatever the successes or failures of the show (and for some it remains the crowning achievement of documentary journalism in Canada), a textual and critical analysis suggests it never achieved a stable and satisfactory portrait of the country for its diverse constituency in the 1980s. Clearly, even the flagship of documentary journalism had trouble producing a nation for television in the later years of public service broadcasting.

CONCLUSION

It is too much to say that Canadian television in its third and fourth decades suffered a "crisis of representation," a term that conjures up images of painful self-reflection and even cultural paralysis. Canadian television never "deconstructed" itself in this way and never stopped trying to represent the nation in the 1970s and '80s. But it is fair to conclude that Canada's chief modes of televised documentary all encountered difficulties representing the country in audiovisual form. Depictions of Canadian private life in vérité television, representations of Canada's past and its hidden present through docudrama, and interpretations and investigations of the day-to-day events and "long durée" of national life in long-form essays and journalistic reports all failed to offer consistently convincing and compelling documentary representations of the nation and its doings.

But despite an apparent exhaustion of the national public service form, documentary was not dead on Canadian television – and Canada was not dead as an object of documentary discourse – as some critics seemed to imply in the genre's later years. In fact, as we shall see, the survival of the form, and its commercial if not cultural renaissance, serve as an interesting case study of Canadian television's remarkable transition from national public service to the global marketplace in the 1990s.

5 Documentary Television Goes Global

Documentary television has generally been regarded as *national* television, in which the nation-state represents its people, places, and issues mostly for the benefit of its own citizen-viewers. Much recent research has further concluded that the genre has little future in a new *global* marketplace, presumably committed to the avoidance of locality, public controversy, and any form of meaning whatsoever in the pursuit of profit. As a sober, nation-bound form, documentary television would seem to have little place in a broadcasting environment dedicated to transnationalism and fun.

How then to explain to explain the recent "phenomenal" success of documentary programming as a worldwide commodity?[1] By 1995 documentaries had come to make up fully 24.4 per cent of international television co-productions, the second highest rate after drama.[2] In Canada documentary production almost tripled in the late 1990s, with most of the programming geared for foreign distribution.[3] By 1998 the genre had become one of Canada's fastest growing cultural exports, according to some observers, with most producers forecasting breakneck growth in the years ahead.[4] Clearly, Canadian documentary television had begun to relocate itself in a global marketplace.

In this chapter I want to consider the causes and consequences of this shift. I begin with an analysis of the *extent* of documentary globalization, that is, of the degree to which Canadian documentary television production and distribution have in fact become transnational in recent years. I then consider the *cultural implications* of globalization, specifically the support the documentary television case lends to cultural nationalist and postmodern scenarios concerning the future of local representation, public investigation, and meaning in global television programming. I conclude with an analysis of two exemplary global documentary texts to further explore these issues.

GLOBALIZED PRODUCTION AND DISTRIBUTION

We should use the term "globalized" with some caution, denoting as it often does a total disarticulation of processes of production, regulation, and reception from any concept of nation-building. Documentary television in Canada has hardly been globalized as such. Canadian documentary was never a purely national project in the first place, and one could argue that transnational production and distribution patterns are really nothing new in Canada. Canada's earliest documentary films were often designed for export and often made by foreign crews, many of them commissioned by the Canadian government and Canadian Pacific Railways to encourage immigration.[5] The country's first broadcast documentaries were similarly produced with exports in mind, with the Canadian Radio Broadcasting Commission in its first year establishing a "very satisfactory system of exchange of programs" with the BBC and the major American networks, an exchange that was seen to provide Canada with "valuable publicity" around the world.[6] Documentary exchanges were arranged for television as early as 1953, beginning with a series of ad hoc agreements between Commonwealth broadcasters and the National Association of Educational Broadcasters (NAEB, the forerunner of the American PBS network) that later developed into the Intertel television treaty involving those countries in the next decade.[7] To be sure, a full-fledged international documentary *market* was hampered by the deliberately parochial nature of most Canadian television at the time,[8] and by Canadian broadcasters' extensive use of 16 mm film formats, which were incompatible with many other countries' television systems.[9] Nonetheless, a solid record of Canadian overseas sales was achieved by documentary programs such as *The Nature of*

Things, *The National Dream*, and in the 1980s, *The Journal* (which in an average year had twenty-five of its documentary reports picked up by the BBC alone.)[10]

Production was also internationalized to some extent. Television's very first international co-productions were documentary programs jointly produced by the BBC and the NAEB in the early 1950s, part of an arrangement that later came to include Canada.[11] International documentary production never received much official support at the time, Canada's first co-production treaties in the 1960s being largely concerned with feature films rather than informational television. But as in the area of distribution, informal international cooperation did take place, with magazine shows such as CBC's *Tuesday Night* and Radio-Canada's *Champ libre* regularly putting together stories with their European counterparts,[12] and Canadian and foreign networks often collaborating on special series such as the *Second World War* (1974) series co-produced with Thames Television.

None of this really amounted to globalization. Co-productions and export projects in the early years of Canadian television were small-scale and often half-hearted. Foreign income from all Canadian film and television productions amounted to only Can$ 6 million between 1955 and 1960,[13] and Canada's isolation from the global market was virtually institutionalized. In the early 1960s documentary producers were still being advised by their supervisors "not to put foreign audience considerations ahead of our own,"[14] and even later in the decade, when overseas sales potential had become an "increasingly important object of [documentary] production"[15] and co-productions were starting to be seen as a "viable way" of dealing with the rising program costs,[16] international production was often seen to involve more problems than it was worth. First and foremost, documentary programmers were reluctant to relinquish editorial control; the CBC's director of information programming, Knowlton Nash, for instance, recounted a series of unhappy experiences with private broadcasters such as Time-Life Television in this regard.[17] Moreover, foreign sales meant that the rights to archive material had to be renegotiated internationally and extra export prints made from available film stock, a difficult and costly process well into the 1970s. While CBC officials continued to urge that information programs be repackaged to "break into the syndication field,"[18] they also acknowledged the "difficulty of selling [overseas] programs planned and produced to the parameters of the CBC."[19]

Thus globalization was found to be largely incompatible with national public service regimes of production, regulation, and distribution. Moreover, existing export and co-production deals were essentially designed to serve state-cultural rather than global-commercial purposes. Documentary exchanges would allow for "national cultures to be represented [by public service broadcasters] to the rest of the world," as one of the Intertel treaties put it.[20] All in all, information television was tentatively internationalized but never globalized in a full-fledged sense and, as a result, documentary programming remained a national public service form in its first three decades.

If we were to fix a "global moment" for documentary television, it would be somewhat later, in the mid-1980s when its reorientation towards a transnational marketplace was bound up with a more widespread globalization of Canadian television in general. As Paul Attallah has noted, the 1980s saw the influx of new production methods and styles in Canadian television, and a general upheaval in the industry.[21] Independent producers began to make programs that were more exportable than their public service predecessors, while specialty channels in Canada and abroad offered a ready exhibition platform for the new shows. The new market was further helped along by regulatory agencies such as Telefilm Canada, which worked to reposition Canadian television as an export-oriented cultural industry, and by new digital technologies that allowed for faster production and easier program distribution across borders. Finally, a cheaper Canadian dollar and the North American Free Trade Agreement attracted further foreign investment and opened up new television export markets (while undermining traditional national cultural protections.)[22] One widely quoted statistic suggests that Canada had actually become the world's second largest television exporter by the end of the decade.[23]

How then would documentary television fare in a new global cultural environment? Or to be more precise, how would a genre essentially mandated to represent national places to national citizens fare in a world of dispersed transnational audiences? And how would a program form ostensibly dedicated to pedagogy and the disciplining of a "one channel audience" survive in a market of unruly channel-hoppers? For most researchers, the answers were simple. According to media economists such as Hoskins and McFadyen, programs representing particular places would be globally unpopular, or at least subject to a high "cultural discount" – that is, diminished appeal as they crossed borders.[24] Public service advocates took a similarly pessimistic line. Robert McChesney and Edward Herman, for instance, insisted that shows dealing with controversial social issues would be largely anathema to global advertisers, just as they had been with American sponsors in an earlier commercial age.[25] All in all, a wide variety of media researchers on both the left and the right agreed that documentary programming would have a hard time making the transition from national public service to a global marketplace. For most, documentary television was an anachronism in a global market, fundamentally at odds with the emerging transnational and commercial aspects of the new media age.

In every respect, the success of documentary television in the global markets of the 1990s was a theoretical anomaly, and a worldwide one at that. In Britain, for instance, five of the BBC's top fourteen program exports in 1994 were documentaries, while in the U.S. the genre enjoyed a "remarkable renaissance," according to *Broadcasting and Cable* magazine, because of the growth of cable and a "love affair throughout the medium and throughout the world with reality-based programming."[26] In Canada, the genre's resurgence was even more spectacular and more globally oriented, with production growing over 270 per cent between 1994 and 1997 by some estimates, the vast majority of that production primarily geared for foreign markets.[27] Market data from around the world thus suggested that documentary was more than able to compete beyond its borders in the new market age.

What factors made documentary television go global in Canada? Some were neither genre nor place-specific, and involved broader market factors. Like TV producers around the world, Canadian documentarists found that deregulated multi-channel markets hardly supported production the way state cultural institutions had. In fact Canadian broadcasters provided most documentaries with only one quarter of their net budgets in 1998, forcing more and more producers to go outside the country for top-up (and sometimes core) funding.[28] Co-productions offered producers average budgets of between Can$ 400,000 and 600,000, approximately triple those of their domestically funded counterparts in 1997.[29] Because of these circumstances, fully 84 per cent of producers sought some form of global financing in 1998,[30] and in this respect documentary production simply went the way of television production in general at the end of the twentieth century.

But beyond being swept up in new millennial markets, documentary productions were arguably *intrinsically global*, or at least particularly attractive to investors with an eye on transnational sales. Documentary costs were relatively low by television standards, the average budget of a one hour show at France's 1998 "Marche des programmes internationales" being just Can$ 350,000 compared to $1.2 million for dramas.[31] Documentaries also offered rebroadcast opportunities unlike other types of information programming such as news and current affairs, and tended overall to be more flexible export commodities. Higher shooting ratios in documentary programming, for instance, produced extra footage that could be re-edited and repackaged for various world markets, while longer gestation periods allowed for further "multiple versioning." In short, investors found documentary programs almost ideally suited to transnational commercial television, market theory notwithstanding.

Moreover, the genre thrived as a result of a larger globally interconnected distribution system. Documentary specialty channels such as the u.s.-based Discovery Network, the History Channel, and Arts and Entertainment, and European counterparts such as France's Planet channel and Spain's Documania established global operations in the late 1980s and '90s for which they sought programs from around the world. Discovery Networks International, the world's largest originator of documentaries, commissioned over 1,800 hours of programming in 1998, while Arts and Entertainment acquired 900 hours of programs the same year, including more than 130 episodes of *Biography*. News channel CNN also planned to invest more heavily in the genre by acquiring 200 hours of programming a year by 2000.[32] New distribution systems, including a 1996 Can$ 1.5 billion co-venture between the BBC and Flextech, were expected to create a dozen new global documentary channels in the near future. These now include the u.s.-based Documentary Channel, reserved for independent productions and established in 1999, and new documentary webcasting services such as the European vivendi.net, established in 2001.

Above and beyond providing access to new consumers, satellite distribution systems *created* new documentary markets in seemingly

unprofitable areas. For instance, Canadian producers had traditionally found even dubbed documentary programs hard to sell in Latin
America because of that region's insitutionalized telenovela tradition
and its unreceptive geography and demographics – a varied, disconnected market of eighteen countries with mostly low income and less-
educated populations. New pan-Latin channels such as Discovery's
South American operations, however, allowed Canadian producers
to reach the homes of upper middle-class viewers, by most accounts
documentary's natural audience. Other channels such as Time-
Warner's Mundo Ole focused on "salsa" productions, and through
them Canadian producers found a new market for both nature and
"disastertainment" shows aimed at a wider demographic.[33]

Finally, documentary television was able to go global because it
never was what its critics and supporters said it was: a purely
instructional genre with intrinsically local appeal. Documentary
programming, as we saw in chapter 3, never functioned as a "pure"
public service form in this way, designed as it was to instruct *and*
involve viewers of various cultural backgrounds in a "middle
ground" sort of way. In short, documentary was able to go global
not just because of financial pressures and global market opportunities, but because of its long-term mutability and adaptability, at
least in its Canadian broadcasting incarnations.

THE IMPLICATIONS OF GLOBALIZATION

But the really interesting question here is not just *whether* or *why*
documentary television in Canada has gone global, but *how* – that
is, with what cultural implications? How would the programs
themselves change in a transnational market, for instance? And
more important, what would be the impact on their objects of
representation, on people and communities around the world?
There are a number of ways of considering these issues, but in
Canada debates have generally revolved around the following questions. First, would globally oriented documentary programs continue to *represent the nation*, given their more transnational
conditions of production and distribution? And even if they did,
would the new programs allow for *public discussions*, given their
market conditions and their relative freedom from traditional
public service obligations? And finally and more generally, would

the documentaries continue to *mean* anything at all in a postmodern world of freely circulating sounds and images? In the sections that follow, I address each of these questions in necessarily speculative terms drawing on whatever statistical, archival, and textual evidence is available in each area.

GLOBAL DOCUMENTARY AND THE REPRESENTATION OF PLACE

First the question of global documentary and place: that is, will documentary television continue to represent national locales in a transnational marketplace, and if so in what way? For many contemporary nationalists the answers are simple and disturbing. Canada is threatened by a lack of effective global representation, the argument goes, with the nation itself in danger of disappearing entirely from global television screens,[34] or else surviving as an empty signifier in a new global "mediascape," a world that represents everywhere in general but nowhere in particular.[35] "If you go to New York and say we've got this great idea and it involves Kenora, Ontario," explains documentary producer Martyn Burke, "they're going to look at you blankly and say, 'If you can add Peoria as well as Kenora, then we'll be happy.' My question is, are we going to be able to do anything Canadian or is [Canada] going to be this 'nowhere land.'"[36] "What we're starting to see," adds producer John Kastner, "is a new generation of filmmakers doing things like *The Plague Monkeys* [a 1996 Canadian co-production concerning the West African ebola plague] as opposed to Canadian stories because they're easier to get made and easier to sell."[37]

We should note at the outset that there is no textual evidence, beyond the anecdotal, to support the notion that Canada and other nations have either vanished or "blended together" on contemporary global TV screens; at least, there has been no systematic content analysis or even in-depth semiotic research to back up such a claim. But for many critics, placeless or generic documentary programs are the logical outcome of a system of production and distribution that comes close to bypassing the nation and its cultural institutions altogether. As producer Michael Kott argues, "With different task masters each wanting a different film, you end up making homogenous mush that looks pretty."[38] Critics have pointed out that all the conditions for a "mush market" seem to be in place in

Canada. Foreign investment in Canadian documentary programs, for instance, has increased quite dramatically – from Can$4.042 million in 1991–93 to $6.038 million in 1993–5.[39] Perhaps more disturbingly, the amount of Canadian money backing these productions – and presumably the degree of Canadian control over their content – is relatively small compared to other genres, constituting just 40 per cent of documentary budgets against 54 per cent of those of their dramatic counterparts.[40]

There are few regulatory controls that might contain the effects of globalization by grounding these productions in a specific Canadian place. The Canadian Television Fund promises to give priority to projects dealing with themes and/or events that are "relevant to Canadians," making "prominent use of Canadian experts, knowledge, talent, opinions or concepts." But at the same time, the fund's organizers have promised to use a "flexible approach" to enforce even these loose requirements,[41] and as of yet they have been rather vague about what they mean by "Canadian" documentary in the first place – chair Richard Stursberg described a Canadian production as one which, "were you to look at it you would have no doubt that it was made by and for Canadians."[42] As Doug Saunders has noted, Canadian content is seen to be recognizably Canadian because a Canadian would recognize it, thereby leaving producers with a tautology but not much of a guide for producing Canadian content.[43] Not surprisingly, critics insist that foreign-funded programs with few regulatory obligations can never be counted on to represent Canada in an accurate or authentic way.

For market advocates, there are just as many reasons to believe that Canada *will* continue to be represented in the new marketplace. Documentary producer Simcha Jacobivici maintains that many Canadian filmmakers continue to think locally as they pitch globally in the documentary market. Canadian production companies often gain more editorial control over their programs by seeking only "final chunks" of funding outside Canada, once tax credits, government funds, and domestic broadcast windows have been secured, thus approaching the global market from a "position of strength," as Jacobivici puts it.[44] Further, many producers claim to be seeking only like-minded partners; Toronto's Assocated Producers recently entered into a permanent co-production deal with

Britain's Channel Four which it claims involves absolutely no relinquishment of Canadian control or sacrifice of Canadian content. Even if we don't take these categorical claims of cultural sovereignty at face value, the straightforward equation of global financing with placeless content may be too simplistic.

Not only have cultural nationalists underestimated the survival skills of Canadian producers, say their critics: they have misread the investment strategies of global buyers. There is in fact little evidence to suggest that the buyers and distributors of documentary programs are working to eliminate cultural specificity in the way that some nationalist accounts suggest. Global documentary channels rarely seek just *one* type of program about *one* type of place for *one* general audience. Instead, like the Discovery Channel, they tend to look for a "range of programs and styles" concerning a "variety of subjects and places" around the world, with "as much cross-over and spin-off potential as possible"[45] – if only because they realize there is more money to be made from a diverse documentary portfolio than from a global repertoire. Most other global buyers make similar claims for the diversity and local specificity of their schedules. National Geographic International, for example, buys documentaries on the assumption that "national audiences demand a reflection of their own regions,"[46] and the Animal Planet channel "consult[s] closely with regional affiliates before arranging acquistions."[47] Even small-scale producers in notoriously generic subgenres such as "adventure documentary" seem to be striving for at least the appearance of local colour in their work. Real Action Pictures of Calgary, for instance, offers not just the "best action footage from around the world" but also a degree of "culture and history" from each locale – something "beyond pure adrenalin," as CEO James Angrove has said.[48] If anything, then, an analysis of production and distribution patterns in the global documentary market bears out not the cultural nationalist nightmare of "placelessness," but a somewhat more complex scenario of "glocalization" in which globalized cultural networks, as Simon During puts it, "paradoxically produce more and more locally produced and consumed goods."[49]

But the question remains: what are these national "places" that global producers and distributors seem so keen to represent? Critics like Martyn Burke may be wrong about places disappearing or only surviving as generic traces on global television screens, but still right to insist that effective national representation – and with it national identity – is jeopardized in a global market. There is in fact a good deal of evidence to suggest that place, whatever its current profile in particular genres or markets, has assumed an altogether more precarious status in global documentary texts than it did in the age of public service. Take "Canada" as represented in the 1997 CTV miniseries, *The Bay*, which recasts the history of the Hudson's Bay Company as an international story set in Montreal, Winnipeg, the Orkney Islands, and London, England.[50] Or take "Ontario" in John Kastner's *Hunting Bobby Oatway*, which under pressure from prospective American investors was almost eliminated even as a story backdrop to make way for a human interest-crime feature about a child molester – until Kastner took the film to the CBC and remade it as an analysis of the provincial justice system.[51] In these cases, Canada serves as a functional and peripheral space in a global text but hardly remains a place to be represented for its own sake.

There are many similar examples. In nature, sports, and entertainment documentaries "Canada" often appears as a commodity sign used to promote a variety of goods and services – in the case of Real Action Pictures' *Extreme Sports*, a line of outdoor gear ("shown to very good advantage in the Rockies," according to CEO Angrove)[52] and in Marco and Mauro LaVilla's *Hang the DJ* (1998), an array of clothing accessories, soundtracks, and even world-touring rave parties all with a "Canadian vibe."[53] In the promotional literature of the Bureau du film du Quebec and the Saskatchewan Film and Video Development Corporation, on the other hand, Canada itself emerges as a sort of simulacrum, filling in for (mythic) places around the world – offering international documentary location scouts everything from a "touch of Europe" in the case of Quebec to Saskatchewan's "five distinct climatic zones ranging from arctic to semi-arid desert."[54] In such cases Canada seems to have neither disappeared nor survived as a fixed signifier with stable meanings. Rather it has *re-emerged*, as Jody Berland has put it in another context, as a "dispensable token susceptible to the requirements of commercial exchange."[55] In short, if cultural nationalist theories of "placelessness" remain unsubstantiated and largely implausible, so do market models suggesting a straightforward grounded representation of locality in a global age.

GLOBAL DOCUMENTARIES AND
PUBLIC DISCUSSION

There is just as little evidence to support either cultural nationalist or global market scenarios concerning the future of public discussion in a global documentary age. The arguments for both sides are by now familiar in form if not detail. Cultural nationalists have generally assumed that documentary diversity, freedom of speech, and "depth" – that is, program content of collective importance to citizen-viewers – can only be provided by public service broadcasters domestically, and by an orderly exchange between public service broadcasters at the international level. In this respect, arguments have changed little since the early 1960s when the Intertel organization declared that a "wider understanding of world affairs and problems" could only be achieved through "an exchange of [public service] documentary television programs."[56] For most cultural nationalists, public discussion, like the representation of place, can be reliably achieved only within the confines of the nation state and its cultural institutions.

For market advocates, on the other hand, genuinely public representation is predicated quite squarely on a system of communication that bypasses the nation state at almost every turn. Documentary programming, in this view, is best supplied by a market of independent producers and globally oriented specialty distributors, largely relieved of national regulatory restrictions and quotas and free to pursue their own "*weltanschaaung*," as former Discovery Channel CEO Trina McQueen puts it.[57] Canada's fledgling documentary industry is by most accounts just such a free market, made up as it is of over four hundred independent producers who promise to introduce new styles and cultural perspectives to the documentary form.[58]

Neither school of thought has much to recommend it empirically. There is little evidence to suggest that public discussion, even of the sort advocated by cultural nationalists, has entirely disappeared in the wake of the public service-dominated broadcasting system. Statistics Canada data in fact suggests that social issue documentaries have done quite well in a deregulated Canadian market, and increased in number compared with softer infotainment forms (though these categories seem to be based on the rather unclear definitions of Canadian producers themselves).[59] Forecasts of a decline of the "serious" documentary are further hampered by a good deal of confusion on all sides concerning what a "serious" documentary *is*.

There are even more reasons to be sceptical of free market models, at least in their more simplistic versions. First and perhaps most problematically, independent productions are hardly independent – and Canadian documentary work hardly "free" – in a Canadian-global market. Precise data in this area is lacking, due to the reluctance of the production sector to reveal ownership and investment information except where required by funding agencies, but it appears that more and more independent companies and exhibition venues are being purchased both by larger production conglomerates and established television networks. The CTV network's proposed purchase of NetStar Communications Incorporated, home of the Canadian Discovery Channel, is but one case in point. Moreover, this trend can be expected to continue if the networks receive permission from the CRTC to buy independent production companies eligible for government funding, a recurring demand from Canadian broadcasters who now seem to want to *own* Canadian programs and sell them on global markets, rather than *license* them in exchange for limited domestic ad revenues.

In a "free" documentary market, then, independents may well be crowded out of the production business by information conglomerates. Indeed, the process may already be underway, with networks and specialty channels soaking up more and more government funding, for instance, by using affiliated companies to access their quota of 33 per cent of Canadian Television Fund monies, and triggering, through their commissions from independents, fully 87 per cent of the same fund in 1998.[60] If anything, government policies designed to encourage diverse and independent work have *increased* monopoly production. Such policies give priority to larger broadcaster-connected firms which are able to invest a substantial amount of their own capital in productions, and which have already received a primetime scheduling commitment from a domestic or international broadcaster.[61] As a result, funding agencies such as the CTF and the various provincial film development offices often make independent firms more dependent, acting like "banks," as one observer puts it, "looking more favourably on investment projects, especially those with international partners."[62] Free of effective policy guidance, the Canadian documentary television industry has increasingly taken the shape of a Hollywood studio system, with large (often vertically integrated) production houses affiliating themselves with established network conglomerates, and a number of smaller producers still in business but mostly dependent on these players.[63] This is hardly a model market for documentary free speech.

Even when smaller companies remain formally independent, free and diverse production may be constrained in less tangible ways. Paradoxically, documentary diversity may be *compromised* by the extraordinary number of documentaries being produced in today's market. The specialty channels' voracious demands for programming, coupled with their pathetically low licence payments (topping off at $50,000 per documentary hour in 1998),[64] force producers to turn out "product" at a speed that critics maintain precludes either creativity or critical self-reflection. Episodes for the Discovery Channel's *The Body: The Inside Story*, to cite just one example, took only three weeks each to produce, from the first day of shooting to delivery, compared with what might have been the six-month gestation period of a comparable public service production. In such a market many producers admit they must "decide what the story is going to be ahead of time, write it, get the experts and add the pictures because it is easier to shoot that way."[65] CBC executive producer Mark Starowicz agrees: "I don't mean to imply that work of depth and diversity is not being done, but the nature of the business is that if you're running one of these little companies, you need the volume, your budgets are stretched, you don't have the money to buy proper archival footage. I know a lot of producers who say they would love to do more ambitious projects but can't."[66]

Documentary diversity and free speech may be further compromised by the rigid format requirements of conventional broadcasters and the specialty channels. Independent producer Barri Cohen, for instance, claims the genre has been effectively "pathologized," with networks demanding programs that "fit into journalistic policies or [are] exactly 43 minutes long."[67] In today's market, then, documentary programming may be less and less capable of dealing creatively with matters of public concern. Indeed "diversity" is somewhat of a misnomer here, with specialty channels seeking a sort of "rationalized eclecticism" in which program tastes and types are effectively defined and contained within commercially convenient categories – within a more or less fixed specialty channel "slot." Even Vision TV, by reputation the most comprehensive, flexible, and public service oriented player in the field, insists on programs that fit its self-styled "hatch, match and dispatch" mandate.[68]

So far we have been discussing constraints on documentary production in Canadian markets. But one might argue that diversity and freedom of expression become even more precarious when programs get into the hands of global buyers and distributors. Simply speaking, there are no firm institutional supports for documentary free speech in a global marketplace – certainly none approximating those which public service producers could (more or less) count on in national television systems. True, there are some basic international conventions that might preserve the *foundations* for public discussion: for instance, the 1936 Geneva Convention on Propaganda, the 1952 Geneva Convention for the Right of Correction, various UN conventions designed to protect journalists, and perhaps most notably, the 1948 Universal Declaration of Human Rights, which asserts everyone's right to to receive and impart information through every medium and across every border. All of these regulations are designed to ensure, if not a transnational "public sphere," at least some minimal insurance that global citizens will be relatively well informed and not incited to kill each other.

But even in this limited sense, international regulation has clearly had little practical effect on international communication in general and documentary programming in particular over the last fifty years. And there is every reason to believe that Canadian documentary programs will be subject to many of the restrictions and few of the protections of both national and international communication policies in a global market. According to many documentary producers, legal and regulatory restrictions tend to be stricter in a global marketplace, because satellite carriers favour programs that meet the national security and obscenity standards of each and every one of their target markets. Similarly, copyright laws tend to be more restrictive, because Canadian producers are forced to secure worldwide rights for file footage and even consider foreign trademarks when titling their productions (as witnessed by the American A&E channel's recent lawsuit against a Canadian company for using the title "Biography" for a documentary series). In short, global distribution systems frequently impose more stringent "community standards," copyright constraints, and overall limitations on documentary speech than do national systems subject to public policy dictates – and importantly, these standards are now enforced by remote and sometimes unaccountable private organizations. As a case study, documentary television thus hardly suggests that public communication will be particularly free in a global post-policy age.[69]

Where then should we look for public discussions in the new documentary marketplace? We might start with the national public service broadcasting sector, which remains quite significant as a source of financing and distribution for documentaries around the world. Internationally, for instance, the European Media Program has worked to establish a regional documentary network, lending money and production facilities to independent companies and aiding them in their search for viable co-production deals.[70] Similarly, the Scandinavian Broadcasting System, merged in 1995 with the Central European Media Enterprises, has created a network of eighteen mostly public service stations that is now the third largest documentary program buyer in the world .[71] Coupled with bilateral agreements between broadcasters like PBS and the BBC, these new arrangements promise to extend the reach of public service programming around the world.

The CBC has tried to maintain its own global profile by producing and distributing programs in entirely new ways. To boost exports, it has begun to experiment with human interest stories and universal themes, fighting, as Starowicz says, for a "place for documentary in this most Darwinian of North American [and international] broadcast markets."[72] The corporation has also made all types of global distribution deals, securing a slot on the U.S.-based DirecTV satellite service, for instance (via the Newsworld International Network), which will allow shows such as the *fifth estate* and *Undercurrents* to be seen by up to 2.5 million American viewers.[73] As part of a more transnational production strategy, CBC has also made a number of big-budget programs with public and private broadcasters around the world, including *Dawn of the Eye* (1996), produced in conjunction with the BBC and Britain's Channel 4. Meanwhile, at home, the corporation has apparently emulated European public broadcasters by offering more "daring and diverse" documentary shows, introducing regular primetime slots for independent long-form documentaries through its *Witness* and *Rough Cuts* series. The latter program, according to its guidelines, is dedicated to airing "creative new perspectives not always visible in mainstream TV journalism."[74]

But for all that, Canada's public service broadcaster hardly offers a full-fledged "alternative space" for documentaries in a global market. In the view of some critics, the CBC lacks a domestic base from which to expand globally because it no longer functions as a major documentary producer at home. As Starowicz sadly notes, "[A] decade ago, CBC News had ten documentary teams whose assignments were geared to the national news agenda. Today there are none."[75] Even as a commissioner, the corporation has become something of a minor Canadian player, with its budgets and its audience shares seemingly caught in a steady inexorable decline.[76]

Public expression has been further constrained by the CBC's own peculiar programming strategies. Diversity has been limited by its recent concentration on documentary "mega-projects" such as *Canada: A People's History* (2000). The series' two-year effective monopoly of public service documentary resources has been described by some independent producers as more of a "dictatorship than an anthology."[77] Freedom of expression has been constrained by the CBC's continued adherence to traditional rules regarding fairness, balance, and accessibility, which still require point of view and regional programmers to attract the interest and appease the sensibilities of viewers across the country. These restrictions are, according to some critics, as severe as they ever were at the CBC. For all its promises to "open doors for productions in diverse parts of the country" and "take risks with newcomers," for instance, the independent documentary showcase *Rough Cuts* still insists that directors "explore themes crucial to all Canadians" and adhere to "traditional CBC editorial [standards of] journalistic excellence."[78] The commissioning process at *Witness* is similarly seen by some critics to be plagued by "excessive caution and buck-passing."[79]

There are, of course, "alternatives" to national public service broadcasting. Provincial public broadcasters, for instance, have provided long-term and mostly steady support for independent documentary production in Canada; TVOntario, for instance, hired Rudy Buttignol, the co-founder of the Independent Film Caucus, to commission long-form point-of-view documentaries from Canada and around the world, for the programs *The Human Edge* and *The View from Here*. The latter show re-edited just three films in its first six years on the air, with Buttignol appearing on panel phone-in shows each time to explain the cuts.[80] Like all forms of "alternative" television, however, provincial public broadcasting is never entirely "free" of the broadcasting and cultural environment of which it is a part. TVO, for instance, was placed on a provincial government privatization list in 1995 with its future as a public broadcaster still very much in in doubt. In the meantime, Buttignol acknowledges "indirect [government] influence on the documentary commissioning process" because of "worries [within the organization] about the government that funds us."[81]

Other "alternatives" – both to public broadcasting and the market – are the growing number of Canadian organizations and cooperatives dedicated to non-network and non-professional modes of documentary programming. Toronto's Channel Zero plans to build a cooperative web of of media stations in developing countries that "ultimately empowers both the organization as well as the host community," creating a media culture which is "global and participational in construct."[82] Public service broadcasting is entirely redefined in such a model, with Channel Zero's "public" united mostly by attitude rather than geography ("the young and pissed off of the earth," as founder Stephen Marshall would have it) and its "service" consisting mostly of cross-generic programs drawing freely on music video styles rather than conventional information forms. "This is free communication," explains Marshall, by which he seems to mean communication with "liberated" signifiers, empowering the communities it is meant to be "about."[83]

Channel Zero, in fact, illustrates both the possibilities and the problems facing independent documentary networks across Canada. Critics have pointed out that the organization is hardly "alternative," dependent as it is on corporate support and network airtime (receiving offers of help from Time-Warner and some slots on the CBC's *National Magazine*, for instance).[84] Further, it is hardly "institutionalized," maintaining no permanent producers of its own in the field and distributing most of its programs not "by channel" but by a haphazard (and generally unprofitable) system of video sales. Neither is it "transnational," failing as yet to build a cooperative network or even a set of mobile stations in the developing world. Nor is it "postmodern" or "postrepresentational," delivering according to even its more sympathetic critics mostly polemics and propaganda in its various video programs.[85] But if Channel Zero is not itself the first organization to "exploit the democratic possibilities of the medium," as Mark Kingwell, a philosophy professor at the University of Toronto, once claimed, it still serves as a valuable (if cautionary) case study of the challenges and potential rewards facing Canada's post-public service documentary broadcasters in a global age.

In short, taking into account the problems and possibilities facing Canada's new documentary producers, public communication can best be seen as conceivable but conditional in a globally oriented media market. Neither cultural nationalist nor market advocate models help us make sense of this environment, offering at least in their most apocalyptic and optimistic versions all-or-nothing scenarios in which public expression either disappears or survives intact in a global age. But in a post-national market, matters are not so simple. Free of both traditional policy restrictions *and* institutional supports, spaces of documentary expression have taken on shifting and ambiguous forms that seem to defy fixed categories.

DOCUMENTARY MEANING IN A GLOBAL AGE

There remains one further outstanding question regarding documentary television in a global age. That is, beyond representing places and public issues, will the genre continue to mean anything at all in a post-public service era? Will it continue to reflect and make sense of the world in at least a minimally coherent and objective fashion?

The arguments that it will not, like those cited above, rest not so much on an analysis of program texts but of the way they are produced, distributed, and viewed in Canada and around the world. Production studies are certainly suggestive in this regard, there being many examples of Canadian documentarists apparently constructing programs out of signs with no obvious referents in the world at large. According to one producer, "no one had shot a frame of [nature] footage for years" in Canada because of the high costs of production, with producers simply recycling images of "Eisenhower-era llamas" for generic wildlife shows in foreign markets.[86] While such practices seem to be frowned upon today, new digitalized production methods allow producers to "fake" it in other ways, for example, by generating computerized images as ostensibly real-life documentary material. (A case in point is the superimposed backdrops used for many of the scenes in *Canada: A People's History.*) In short, the new technologies and economies of documentary television seem to be undermining the evidentiary value of much of its programming.

Producers have also shown less and less inclination to organize these "real life" sights and sounds within orderly generic boundaries. In Canada, fact and fiction styles have become increasingly blurred, giving rise to new stylistic mutations such as "shockumentaries" and "sexumentaries." CITY-TV's *SexTV*, History Television's 1997 miniseries *The Sexual Century*, and the WTN channel's *Private Dicks: Men Exposed* (1999) are recent cases in point, the latter program, according to critic John Doyle, consisting of "a bunch of men being deadly serious about their dicks."[87] This trend has apparently even worked its way into traditionally staid sub-genres such as the nature show, which according to the president of Rhombus International productions "contains a lot more sex now."[88] In a truly bizarre fusion, WTN has even launched *Cooking for Love,* a "documentary/comedy/cooking show" whose host spends a day shopping and cooking with grandmothers of different ethnicity across Canada.[89] Canadian producers thus seem to be disregarding not just the traditional moral and cultural hierarchies of Canadian documentary television but virtually any representation categories whatsoever in their search for marketable formats.

If that's not enough, meaningless – or at least disorderly – representation may be compounded at the distribution and exhibition level. Here documentary texts are often "sliced and diced" to fit broacast schedules or the perceived tastes of target markets. Textual coherency may be undermined as the programs are loosely grouped into commerically convenient but not always coherent line-ups. History Television, for instance, offers an information-entertainment package of documentaries, feature films, and reality TV shows, with each format designed not to stand alone but to contribute to a sort of nightly "historical experience," according to vice-president Norm Bolen.[90] With most of these programs and schedules intended to appeal to a general interest as opposed to a specialist viewer, offering a sort of one-stop culture shopping, the past on Canadian television seems to be offered not as a meaningful body of knowledge but as a generalized source of pleasure.[91]

Documentary programs may become even less meaningful as they are juxtaposed and jumbled together by viewers at home. It seems reasonable to assume that in a multi-channel remote control universe, viewers will "zap" and "station hop" programs to create their own personalized documentary (slash/whatever) "texts," thereby further undermining whatever textual integrity the programs had in the first place. In such conditions documentary meaning would appear to lie in ruins.

Compelling as they can be, such models remain almost entirely speculative, and rather implausible when examined more closely. While information concerning documentary audiences is scarce in Canada, survey data from other countries suggest they may be more selective and sedentary – and thus perhaps more "sensible" – than other types of TV viewers.[92] Just as problematically, postmodern accounts have tended to disregard documentary *distributors* and the ways they work to stabilize audience expectations and program meanings. Distributors may impose a certain order on the programs by selecting only those which complement their line-ups and channel image. CNN's Jennifer Hyde seeks documentaries of a similar length and style, all united by their "relevancy to what is going on in the world" (according to CNN).[93] A&E's Amy Briamonte seeks immediately clear themes, "maximum five-liners which jump out at you from the TV *Guide.*"[94] Both commissioning editors prefer stories that fit into a series format, which can be positioned and made sense of within a larger text. A "free flow" of images is thus less plausible when one takes the documentary channelling processes into account.

Just as buyers impose a certain structure – and perhaps meaning – on shows, new viewer services work to make program content more orderly and predictable at the reception level. The U.S.-based Documall service, for instance, offers its clients customized schedules where shows are categorized according to style and theme, backed up by in-depth review and search engines to help make sense of this material.[95] In Canada the Internet is similarly seen as a means to regulate audiences and the meanings they derive from programs, with documentary websites, according to consultant Tom Johnson, "interlacing show with show, and series with series to draw the audience from place to place within the network brand."[96] With such efforts to counteract the random flow of images and audiences in the new documentary universe, it is at least possible that viewers (like producers) will be less and less inclined to mix and match texts with impunity; the "free play" of documentary meaning may be kept in check by market forces much as it was by regulatory practices in the public service age.

So far we have been considering the way documentary television is produced and distributed in a more global market environment, and the degree to which traditional components of public service representation have survived in the face of these practices. But what about the shows themselves? How is the nation represented in specific documentary programs? How is public discussion facilitated (or thwarted) and how is the world made sense of for documentary viewers? By taking a closer look at specific documentary texts, we can explore some of these issues in a more grounded, systematic way. The section that follows considers how places, public issues, and meanings actually figure in two globally oriented programs recently shown on Canadian television.

AN EXAMPLE: *SHOOTING INDIANS*

Shooting Indians is a useful show to start with. Ali Kazimi's one-hour documentary, funded and broadcast by TVOntario in 1996, explicitly addresses themes of place, public identity, and meaning in its very first frames. "My journey begins where Columbus's journey was supposed to end," the director announces in his opening voice-over. "Delhi, 1965. We have visitors from England and they have presents for us." As the camera shows a plastic gunfighter in front of a period photo of Kazimi greeting his white guests, he explains, "These are cowboys. They are good. These are Indians," he continues, as a new figure appears. "They are bad." An image of a plastic warrior fades into the opening credits as sitar music begins to well up in the soundtrack, and the body of the program begins.

"Toronto 1983," Kazimi continues. "It's my first year studying film as as student in Canada. Here I am called an East Indian." A photo of the student-director at the time is replaced by a nineteenth-century portrait of a Mohawk chief. "Here I see real red Indians in the turn of the century photography of Edward Curtis. They seduce me," says Kazimi, "because they remind me of Westerns I have seen in India." As he searches for a thesis project for his graduation film, he comes across the work of Jeffrey Thomas, an Iroquois photographer, and in the early 1980s a "struggling artist."

Kazimi decides to make a film about him which eventually – after ten years of stops and starts – becomes *Shooting Indians*.

In Canadian television terms this is clearly an unconventional documentary. First, unlike most public service projects, *Shooting Indians* maintains little distance from – or conventional authority over – its subjects. Relations between producer and source are amicable but contractual. "I liked what you were doing," Thomas tells Kazimi early in the film. "You talked about that sense of being an outsider in Canada, and the kind of problems we both had were parallel ... I don't think I would have been comfortable doing the film with anyone else." Ethnographic authority in fact becomes increasingly problematic throughout the film. Kazimi acknowledges midway that his preoccupation with Thomas's work has made him oblivious to the turmoil in his subject's personal life that forced shooting to come to a halt in the mid-1980s. Thomas constantly renegotiates his own dealings with urban aboriginals, eventually focusing on "tourist events" such as the modern Pow Wow that give him access to the community "without being intrusive." Even Thomas's and Kazimi's relationship with Edward Curtis, nineteenth-century "appropriater" of Native American imagery, becomes complicated as both begin to "unexpectedly" connect with their earlier counterpart and the choices he had to make in the photography markets of the early twentieth century.

Shooting Indians' diasporic concerns further make any public service-type attempts to "represent" a fixed (national or cultural) identity entirely problematic. Both Thomas and Kazimi initially seek to capture an "essence of aboriginality," Thomas working to replace romantic European stereoypes with "real native images," Kazimi coming to Canada in search of the "mythic Red Indian." But both documentarists come to reject these fixed stereotypes and the models of cultural authenticity underlying them. Kazimi argues that "aboriginal cultures, like all including my own, have borrowed and absorbed influences from all cultures, reviving and at times reinventing themselves." In the end, *Shooting Indians'* title emerges as a sort of pun in which traditional documentary work figures as both a mode of recording and an act of symbolic violence. The film opts to portray natives not as "objects of documentation" but as subjects-in-progress whose more or less migrant identities can never be captured by public service-type representations.

How does the nation figure in such a work? Only peripherally, it might seem, as *Shooting Indians* seems far more concerned with diasporic communities and border crossings than with any sort of homeland. Identities, according to the film, cannot be circumscribed geographically or discursively. People who think of themselves as East Indian or Native Indian have migrated across a number of state boundaries and defined themselves in different ways. And while there are a number of unofficial "native lands" they might return to, these are less grounded than the most "strategically ambiguous" places represented in public service documentaries. In *Shooting Indians*, places, including the nation, are valued not as inviolable and ultimately incontrovertible signifiers or reservoirs of meaning but as as mutable "somewheres" one can (but need not) return to to define oneself. "Indians do exist," notes Kazimi, "even if they have no India to return to." Nations and places are thus not so much containers of identity as strategic touchstones for identity formation.

Further, what form of public discussion does such a work allow? *Shooting Indians* hardly offers a conventional type of public affairs discourse in this regard. The film rarely explicitly considers critical issues or possible courses of action for the native community, and with its emphasis on image over narration, and evocative commentary over logocentric discourse, it is hard to imagine such a critical exposition taking place. Moreover, the concerns of the film are not strictly speaking public at all, centred as they are on *personal* journeys culminating in *contingent* identity formations, rather than *collective* discussions resulting in some sort of community *consensus*. There are meeting grounds in *Shooting Indians*, but they are something quite different than a conventional "public sphere."

And what about meaning in Kazimi's work? *Shooting Indians'* preoccupations with shifting boundaries might be dismissed as mere postmodern relativism, but Kazimi seems to want to recuperate some form of "documentary knowledge" here – that is, knowledge dealing with a series of (contingent) "historical truths" that are inaccessible to any single mode of representation. Indian identity, for instance, is neither "reflected" nor "deconstructed" in the film but rather examined indirectly through its contextual resonances – Kazimi's stated aim being not so much to recapture an Indian *past* (through representation) as to activate an Indian *present* (through various forms of confrontation and mediation). "The vanishing Indian race," he claims, "emerges only from the shadows reborn and renewed in its engagement with its own historical depiction." Here documentation is understood not as "cultural representation" or even "debunking," but as a method of *intervention* in a changing world. In all these ways *Shooting Indians* retains but radically redefines the role of place, public discussion, and meaning in Canadian documentary.

ANOTHER EXAMPLE: *OVER CANADA*

Over Canada is a very different sort of text, a high-definition video portrait of the regions of Canada, funded by the Royal Bank of Canada and designed for both domestic and export "travellogue" markets.[97] This may seem to be about as far as from independent point-of-view documentary as one can get. But, like *Shooting Indians,* this program illustrates the continuing but increasingly provisional importance of place, public representation, and meaning in more globally oriented documentary productions.

Over Canada begins with a series of aerial shots of Canada's regions, all accompanied by a folk guitar soundtrack and a narrator who puts these scenes into perspective. "There is a land almost too vast to contemplate," we are told. "Unimaginably vast, a country the size of the world ... a march of endless horizons revealed one upon the next, in relentless breathtaking magnificence. Celebrate a journey of the heart, a journey over Canada."

Over Canada thus begins by imagining the nation in what would seem to be fairly conventional public service terms. Canada is divided into a series of clear-cut regions, each highlighted on a satellite map and then examined in greater detail by an aerial tour in the early fall. Regions themselves are seamlessly woven into a a national whole, with each program segment connecting the waves, beaches, or roads of one area to those of the next, guided by a continuous soundtack. Aerial camerawork consistently follows one direction (straight ahead and slightly to the right) as it proceeds across the country. Moreover, this is a master view of Canada, a portrait of abstract spaces emptied of features that might complicate the picture. Ground level images are rare – and always in motion, following the same direction as the aerial shots – while individual faces and voices are mostly indistinct. *Over Canada* thus offers a high-definition but apparently conventional portrait of Canada as a unified land mass unfolding in a single moment of time.

Also like many documentary essays in the public service age (see chapter 4), *Over Canada* makes sense of its object by apparently "discovering" meaning in the land itself. Canada is presented as a "visual tapestry,"[98] a sort of geographic-semiotic system in which each region is positioned and defined in relation to another. This topographical collage begins with the Maritimes ("majestic, wild, primitive and honest ... music is its soul"); then proceeds to Ontario ("here beats a Canadian heart, here Canada bunches it muscles and clenches its fist in toil"); then out to the Prairies ("open-hearted nurturing Mother Prairie, bustling off and away with such simple-mindedness"); up to the Arctic ("upon much of whose vastness no foot has ever stepped, no eye ever rested"); ending up in British Columbia ("a haunted place where misty fogs cloak ancient spirits"). In these ways *Over Canada* imposes a strict and familiar discursive order on its subject.

But this is hardly an image of Canada one would expect to find on public service television. Most importantly, *Over Canada* lacks any conventional expository structures. There is really no logocentric motor to the program which, apart from the lyrical outbursts cited above, offers its viewers little narrative guidance and hardly even an implicit argument for the unity or essence of its object. *Over Canada* is perhaps most remarkable for its refusal to make sense of Canada in traditional documentary terms. Canada just *is* – a beautiful tapestry but not much else, a view of the country that troubled many Canadian critics at the time of its release. "A whirley bird's-eye view ... a coffee table book on the move," is how critic John Allemang described the show, noting that "a few seconds' glimpse of a forest or a fjord doesn't begin to tell a story."[99]

At the same time, the program does seem to offer its viewers something more than depthless topography. Canada is not simply a "nowhere land." If anything, the program betrays a scrupulous (if peculiar) attention to local detail – with regions and principalities given airtime in accordance with their presumed political weight, and the representation of each conducted in consultation with tourist boards across the country.[100] Moreover, *Over Canada* strives for cultural diversity, including scenes of Wanuskewin Pow Wow in Saskatchewan, the St Jean-Baptiste parade in Montreal, and the Caribana festival in Toronto amongst others. If cultural difference is never substantively addressed or engaged on its own terms, neither is it entirely avoided as one might expect in an export-minded program.

But while place and cultures have hardly disappeared here, they have arguably assumed a very provisional status. According to one co-producer, the show's primary aim is to remind viewers "there is no place like home – we have a fantastic variety of lifestyles, wilderness, and mountains worth looking at."[101] In the words of another, KCTS TV of Seattle, *Over Canada* offers a "stunning visual experience" made possible by "cutting edge high-definition technology" (KCTS being one of the first stations in the U.S. to introduce programming of this type).[102] Cultural context is indispensable for both projects, according to the program's website, as it gives viewers "a real feel for the places they are seeing on screen."[103]

Place and culture thus apparently serve to enhance the value of a tourist site on the one hand, and a consumer technology on the other. "Canada" emerges as a set of places, the meanings of which provide a depth of feeling or sensation, differentiating this space from others in a way that might be attractive to contemporary image shoppers. The nation emerges as a space to be consumed rather than a place to be represented for the people who live there – a spectacle (or "march of horizons") to be returned to for visual pleasure, but hardly a source of meaning to be returned to for "identity" in any conventional sense of that word. As *Over Canada*'s narrator notes at the end of the program, "the true measure of this eternal and glorious Canada exists not in a rock or a place, not in a mountain or a coast or a shield of ice, but in the imaginations it fires and the dreams it nurtures." In these circumstances, it is not just acceptable but entirely appropriate that the program remains, as it does throughout, "over Canada."

CONCLUSION

Documentary programs arguably perform a public service in global age, continuing to represent people, places, and public issues in more or less meaningful ways. At the same time, the traditional components of the public service documentary have assumed a much more provisional status in programs such as *Shooting Indians* and *Over Canada* with places, issues, and meanings being largely contingent and mutable in the first case, and marketable and malleable in the second. In both programs, the mainstays of Canadian public service documentary figure as necessary but to some extent subservient vehicles for evoking sensations and truths no longer grounded in specific locales or ideological positions. Nations have not disappeared from these texts, but they clearly cease to function as *containers* of meaning or identity.

Overall then, the traditional components of Canadian documentary programming have neither survived nor been fully eclipsed in a post-national age. Rather, they seem to have re-emerged in a way that escapes the logic of conventional theories of globalization. In the global age, documentary television's paradigm text is perhaps neither the representative "local community program" nor the "generic human interest piece" (the poster genres of conventional globalization theories), but rather the *travel show*, where specific settings, public issues, and systems of meaning all figure as indispensable but largely instrumental components of a different sort of program altogether – one designed to bring the viewer not "home" but somewhere else entirely, if only for a moment and for whatever the reason. The implications of this documentary shift are further considered in the final chapter.

6 Conclusion

This book has been concerned with three main subjects: documentary television per se, public service broadcasting in Canada, and the thorny issue of cultural globalization. With regard to the first, I have been mostly concerned with rescuing documentary television from the margins of Canadian film theory where it has languished for more than half a century.[1] For several reasons I believe documentary in broadcast form should be treated in more depth and with more respect than it has been in that body of literature. First, it is a *distinct* genre, grounded in its own modes of production, distribution, and consumption (see chapter 2); secondly, it is an *interesting* genre, often as innovative and almost always more popular than documentary cinema in Canada (see chapter 4); finally, it is an *influential* genre, helping to define Canadian television from its national public service to its global market ages (see chapters 4 and 5). This last point is particularly crucial. There may not be a universally accepted golden age of television in Canada but most versions – whether based in the "experimental" period of the 1950 and '60s, in the years of "consolidation" of the 1970s and '80s, or in the globally competitive market of the 1990s and beyond – would feature documentary programming at their core. For all these reasons, documentary television in Canada is a genre worth studying.

My second concern in this book has been to use documentary television as a case study of public service broadcasting, and to call into question the common association of that institution with modern hegemonic culture, which attempts to confine the meanings and pleasures of television within strict liberal-partriarchal and national boundaries. Public service broadcasting, to be sure, is often regarded as modern culture at its most boring – cultural fare that powerful white men have deemed to be good but not necessarily fun for the nation. But a closer look at its defining Canadian genre, in its various "golden ages," suggests that broadcasting as such was the site of endemic struggles concerning not just documentary form and content but the nature and purpose of televisual representation in Canada. Racked by internal and external conflicts, Canada's public service broadcaster seemed unable to deliver clear meanings and predictable pleasures to a disciplined public on any sort of regular basis, even in its years of "cultural monopoly," and is thus best regarded not as an institution where modern hegemonic culture was "installed" but as a site for its partial unravelling in the post-war period.

Finally and relatedly, I have tried to use documentary television as a case study of cultural globalization as it has affected one genre in one country over a certain period of time. Globalization has not been straightforward in Canada. For instance, it has not involved a simple process of postmodernization in which documentary television has moved from an experimental stage into a classical era and then on to a period of parody and pastiche. Deconstructive features were present in some of Canada's earliest documentary programs (see chapter 3); and, by the same token, many "post-representational" programs continue to make sense, though perhaps in more contingent and conditional ways, in the contemporary era (see chapter 5). Nor has documentary globalization involved a clear-cut end of the national project, with Canada proving ever less able (and inclined) to represent itself in televisual terms. This study has not been about the "rise and fall" of a national project as such, but about its transformation in fits and starts, with traditional public service components being not so much "eclipsed" as radically reconfigured in a global cultural age.

Broadly speaking, this book has offered a history of a particular Canadian television genre from 1952 to the present, along with a sustained critique of contemporary theories of cultural institutions and cultural change. I turn my attention now to a number of questions raised by such a study, all revolving around the central issue of whether documentary will continue to perform a public service in a post-national age. Will documentary survive as a recognizable genre? And if so, will it continue to represent places and public issues? And if it does, what will become of its traditional objects of representation, particularly the nation state?

Let me begin with the question of documentary television and its prospects in a global market. Canadians have years of experience pondering, and usually worrying about, documentary's future. Critics in the 1950s focused on the decline of the National Film Board and the cinematic tradition; in the 1960s on the rise of tabloid journalism; in the 1970s and '80s on the decline of independent point-of-view features; and in the 1990s on the rise of placeless (and some said pointless) infotainment hybrid documentary programs. Indeed, if we are to believe the pundits, documentary programming in Canada has been in "serious decline" since its first days on the air. It is thus easy to be smug about the future of the form in a post-national age, if only because we have heard all the doom and gloom before. But that said, I believe documentary programming *does* face substantial new challenges in a global market, and I want to consider some of these in turn.

First there are questions about television as a means of delivering documentary content. Will television continue to be the documentary medium of the next century, the vehicle by which documentary texts are delivered to audiences around the world in a multimedia age? Might TV documentaries, for instance, be replaced by websites, or advanced CD-Rom programs? Or might they survive in almost unrecognizable "post-broadcasting" forms, with even the specialty channels on which they are currently "lined-up" replaced by the thoroughly individualized schedules of the "documall"?

Questions regarding the future of documentary television as we know it are reminiscent of those surrounding documentary film in the early days of television; and though we should never be too sure of a place for old media in a new media age, documentary television arguably has some intrinsic advantages over its cinematic predecessor. First and foremost, television complements its "competitors" in a way documentary film never did: CD-Roms and documalls are as of yet designed to work in conjunction with, rather than in place of, documentary television. As television consultant Tom Johnson notes, "there is no replacement medium on the horizon – television is still the base information medium in most homes and the one to which new media attach themselves at present."[2] As regards post-broadcasting and post-narrowcasting forms which supposedly undermine the whole network infrastructure of documentary programming, present contenders like the documall still customize broadcasting schedules rather than creating new individualized Internet-type networks.

Perhaps of more immediate concern to documentary producers and programmers themselves is the future of *recorded* documentary programming in the so-called "live information" age. According to many observers, the future of documentary is more questionable than that of television itself. This is the age, say the critics, of instant reportage, from the "wall-to-wall" coverage of CNN,[3] to the ubiquitous microviews of the "earthcam" which provides simultaneous links to laundromats, toilets, and even human nostrils around the world.[4] What place is there for *recorded* and *partial* documentary reports in the face of such seemingly *complete, immediate,* and *unmediated* images of the world? Again, at the risk of being sanguine, it is worth remembering that critics have pondered the future of documentary since the earliest days of live television (see chapter 3). But perhaps more to the present point, ratings around the world suggest that the demand for documentary programming is greater than it ever was (see chapter 5). Indeed CNN, the world's largest live information programmer, is heavily banking on the genre, significantly increasing its investment in "investigative reports" in recent years. Again producers and programmers seem to believe that documentary television complements rather than competes with new types of audiovisual information.

Finally, a more philosophical question: What is the future of documentary or any type of reality programming in a postmodern "post-realist" age? Critics have pointed to an unfavourable epistemological shift for documentary television – a declining faith in the TV camera's ability to objectively record events, and an apparent abandoning of the search for televisual truth in a digital simulation age. For some the power and persuasiveness of documentary is diminished in a media-saturated world where images become cheap and only relatively "true."[5] For others, documentary truth is compromised by a proliferation of styles and subgenres often indistinguishable from those of fiction.[6] For still others, new types of computer generation call into question the indexicality of photographic images and thus the epistemological foundations of documentary itself.[7]

Whatever the current reality status of documentary programming amongst academics, existing research seems to indicate a continuing faith in at least contingent forms of documentary truth on the part of both producers[8] and audiences.[9] Viewers' apparent continuing "hunger for the real" may be largely inexplicable within a postmodern paradigm,[10] but as Williams notes, moving images still seems to have the power to "move audiences to a new appreciation of the truth," even if this truth is no longer seen to be a fixed and easily accessible object of representation.[11] Moreover, any discussion concerning documentary epistemology in the global age must take into account (as most postmodern theories do not) continuing on-the-ground efforts by programmers to reinforce meanings, generic categories, and thus "truth" on television (see chapter 5).

Arguably then, documentary television is more or less ready to meet the challenges posed by new technologies, new markets, and new epistemological-cultural formations in the forseeable future. But if documentary has a future in a global postmodern age, can the same be said for its traditional objects of inquiry? We have already noted that places and public issues now figure very differently in documentary texts than they did in the past. But to put the question in stark Canadian terms, can these places and public issues continue to make sense without a supporting system of public policies and public service-type representations? More specifically, can Canada survive in the wake of a national public service age, given its long-time self-declared reliance on documentary culture as a source of identity?

There have been two Canadian schools of thought regarding these questions. For cultural nationalists, as we have seen, a nation that disappears from global television screens is a nation with no political-cultural future at all – a "nowhere land," as one patriotic producer puts it.[12] Nations, particularly marginal nations like Canada, cannot survive, in this view, without continuing and coherent televisual representation of their various places and public issues. There simply can be no nation without documentation.

For market advocates and some cultural theorists, on the other hand, new forms of commodified representation have begun to engender sustainable types of "Canadianness" without the need for public service supports. McLuhan and Powers make a typically cryptic but influential case to that effect, arguing (without reference to any particular genre or market) that global commodified information flows benefit marginalized countries such as Canada – economically, by allowing them to sell themselves as repositories of difference in an increasingly interconnected world, and culturally, by reinforcing their ironic stance towards all forms of fixed national identity and cultural cliché (an irony on which their national identity was founded in the first place). In every sense, then, nations (at least those that don't take themselves too seriously) benefit by selling themselves as documentary stereotypes – as blank slates or receptive "playgrounds" for other people's fantasies.[13] In this view, there *can* be a nation with virtually any form of documentation whatsoever – though apparently the more global, market-oriented, and epistemologically liberated the better.

There are problems with both approaches. As far as documentary television goes, there is good reason to doubt nationalist models as both cultural strategy and cultural theory. To begin with, how can national documentary programming be supported in a global age, through what sorts of policy structures? The Canadian Television Fund, for instance, has been notably unsuccessful in supporting Canadian content and documentary diversity in recent years, favouring big-budget export-oriented companies at the expense of independent local producers (see chapter 5). With some exceptions, nationalist critiques have been conspicuously vague about what is wrong with the CTF and about what might replace it. Even leaving aside the precise institutional logistics, how might Canadians support "national" documentary programming without substantively defining it, guided by something more precise than a generic point system? And how, at the same time, can Canadian authorities define documentary programming as such without confining it within fixed and probably indefensible hegemonic boundaries? On the horns of this dilemma, the cultural nationalist documentary project seems hard to defend and hardly worth defending in a global age.

At the same time, can we really do without any notion of national public service in a global documentary market? The global market may, as its advocates claim, give new life to documentary forms by liberating signifiers from hegemonic restrictions, thereby clearing the way for new types of "affective alliance" and imagined communities around the world. But there is little evidence of this. It is difficult, first of all, to know what a free play of documentary signifiers would look like. For many theorists it would take the form of a new regime (or anti-regime) of representation (or anti-representation) allowing for new types of enunciation and new spaces of subjectivity. For Felix Guattari, such a "system" would in fact be a liberatory apparatus in the fullest sense of the word, based not on individualized but on collective production and consumption, centred not on orderly representation but on the "plenitude of the image," and focused not on identity at all but on difference, diversity, and mutation.[14] But clearly a global documentary market – that is, a system geared towards the production of predictable clichés and fixed (if proliferating) program types – is not what Guattari had in mind. Global market documentary production, as we have seen, involves constant "semiotic policing," subjugating images, subjects, and presumably "libidinal desires" to the laws of profit and economic exchange. Surely a global market is no more predisposed to documentary "free play" than the national public service systems that preceded it.

Might a global documentary market, on the other hand, help realize a more conventional type of "imagined community," one founded not on the deconstruction of public service notions of meaning and identity but rather on their refinement and extension around the world? Might a free market play of documentary images, for instance, encourage new feelings of worldwide interconnectedness and mutual concern, creating what McLuhan called a "global village" and what Anthony Giddens has more recently dubbed a "world with no 'Others'"?[15] We are, of course, literally speculating on a global scale at this point, but it should be noted that existing communication research hardly suggests that free-flowing transnational communication engenders new global communities in a straightforward way. As John Tomlinson has noted, this is not so much because the world is too large to be "connected" (imagined national communities have rarely been inhibited by scale), nor because global populations are too dispersed (diaspora populations often thrive despite distance). The real reason may be that the global village, unlike its national and diasporic counterparts, lacks a developed political culture and cultural infrastructure through which common meanings could be represented.[16]

In short, it is hard to imagine documentary television, on its own or with existing cultural supports, giving rise to a global village like the one McLuhan had in mind. Viewers watching different (versioned) programs at different (often videotaped) times in different (dispersed market) places probably share a preference for similar types of programs, but not much else. In such conditions, isolated from complementary arenas for public life, documentary audiences may find they have little in common with each other or with the people they are watching on screen.

All in all, then, the global documentary market hardly promises new forms of subjectivity or community to replace those engendered by the nation state. A much better case can be made for global documentaries functioning not as public spheres, or even founding texts for new imagined communities, but rather as "spaces of identity"[17] allowing for at least some form of privatized reflexivity – that is, for a monitoring and reshaping of the self in light of available global-cultural choices. Documentary television, in this light, could circulate new models of identity disembedded from place and tradition, thereby making personhood a truly reflexive project in a global age – even if this involves a degree of what Bryan Turner has called "experiential secularity,"[18] a growing sense, in the face of incoming documentary images and possibilities, that we are all tourists at home, occupying but never really belonging to any particular cultural territory. New documentary identities may thus be based not on a grounding of the self in a meaningful place but on its disarticulation from increasingly meaningless locales.

All of this is possible. And certainly worth considering. In an increasingly disorderly and unpredictable global cultural environment, it would be wrongheaded and unrealistic to insist that documentary television in Canada concern itself only with fixed identities grounded in particular national places, all for the sake of narrow and non-negotiable hegemonic cultural purposes. But if the nation state and its citizens and places are no longer the only conceivable objects of documentary representation in a global marketplace, this does not mean they no longer deserve even tactical support, either as valuable documentary components in their own right or as viable cultural counterpoints to market hegemony in a global television age. In this sense, Canadian documentary television's *transition* from national public service to a global marketplace, rather than its arrival at one point or the other, continues to be perhaps its best hope for a new golden age.

Appendix

22. *Living* (CBC) — 1954–55
23. *Man Alive* (CBC) — 1967–
24. *Marketplace* (CBC) — 1972–
25. *National Dream* (CBC) — 1974
26. *The Nature of Things* (CBC) — 1960–
27. *Ombudsman* (CBC) — 1974–80
28. *Open House* (CBC) — 1954–62
29. *Pacific 13* (CBC) — 1956
30. *Public Eye* (CBC) — 1965–69
31. *Quest* (CBC) — 1961–64
32. *Scattering of Seeds* (History Television) — 1997–98
33. *Scope* — 1954–55
34. *SexTV* (CityTV) — 1998–
35. *The Sixties* (CBC) — 1963–66
36. *Sunday* (CBC) — 1966–67
37. *Tabloid* (CBC) — 1953–60
38. *Take 30* (CBC) — 1962–83
39. *Tenth Decade* (CBC) — 1971–72
40. *This Hour Has Seven Days* (CBC) — 1964–66
41. *This Land* (CBC) — 1970–82
42. *This Week* (CBC) — 1973–75
43. *Up Canada* (CBC) — 1973–75
44. *Valour and the Horror* (CBC) — 1992
45. *The Way It Is* (CBC) — 1967–69
46. *Window on Canada* (CBC) — 1953–55
47. *W5* (CTV) — 1966–77, 1978–

SERIES AND MINI-SERIES (TELEVISION)

1. *The Body: The Inside Story* (Discovery Canada) — 1998
2. *The Boys of St Vincent* (CBC) — 1991
3. *Camera on Canada* (CBC) — 1964–6
4. *Canada 100* (CBC) — 1967
5. *Canada's Sweetheart* (CBC) — 1985
6. *The Canadians* (CTV) — 1988
7. *Cooking for Love* (WTN) — 1999–
8. *Hail and Farewell* (CBC) — 1967
9. *The King Chronicles* (CBC) — 1988
10. *Pacific 13* (CBC) — 1957
11. *Remembering Canadians at War* (CBC) — 1998

12. *Spirit of '67* (CBC) — 1966
13. *The Style Is the Man Himself* (CBC) — 1968
14. *Tenth Decade* (CBC) — 1971

SPECIAL PROGRAMS (TELEVISION)

1. *Air of Death* (CBC) — 1967
2. *Carole* (CBC) — 1966
3. *Flight into Danger* (CBC) — 1957
4. "Men Are from Manhattan, Women from Saskatchewan" (CBC Newsworld) — 1999
5. *National Survival* (CBC) — 1959
6. *Open Grave* (CBC) — 1963
7. *The Plague Monkeys* (CBC Newsworld) — 1996
8. *Private Dicks: Men Exposed* (WTN) — 1999
9. "Through a Blue Lens" (NFB, CBC) — 1999
10. "The Trouble with Evan" (CBC) — 1999

DOCUMENTARY PROGRAMS (RADIO)

1. *Canadian Scene* (CBC) — 1954–58
2. *The Craigs* (CBC) — 1939–64
3. *Fighting Navy* (CBC) — 1941–46
4. *Saturday Magazine* (CBC) — 1949–51
5. *In Search of Ourselves* (CBC) — 1948–52
6. *Street Scenes* (CBC) — 1938–40
7. *Theatre of Freedom* (CBC) — 1941–46
8. *Wednesday Night* (CBC) — 1947–63

Notes

CHAPTER ONE

1 Stephen Plumb, "What's in Store for Canadian Television," *Winnipeg Free Press*, 23 September 1952.

2 Ibid.; a sentiment echoed by many contemporary observers of global television. Documentary producer Mark Starowicz argues that a "country which cannot produce its own documentaries on the Middle East or Europe or South America ... is relegated to the role of spectator ... and second-class world citizenship" (Starowicz, "Citizens of Video America: What Happened to Canadian Television in the Satellite Age," in Roger de la Garde, William Gilsdorf and I. Weschellmann, eds., *Small Nation Big Neighbour* [London: John Libbey, 1993], 95).

3 Eugene Hallman, executive vice-president, CBC; *Report*, National Conference: Outside Broadcasts Department, 27 November – 1 December 1961, Appendix B: 26; CBC National Archives Papers, RG 41, series A-V-2, vol. 851, PG1-13, pt. 3.

4 Morris Wolfe, *Jolts: The TV Wasteland and the Canadian Oasis* (Toronto: James Lorimer, 1985), 78.

5 Canadian Television Fund, "Funding Cycle Complete," 28 May 1999 Press Release: 1.

6 Consider also Hallman's assertion that "Canada alone has recognized the need to use television to reflect a distinct way of life,"

assuming that Canadians must televisually document themselves *because they are different*, while at the same time being different *because they document themselves* (Hallman, *Report*, 28). Documentary television has always assumed a heavy rhetorical burden in Canadian cultural discourse.

7 Harold Metsem, "Hot Docs Fest in the Works," *Playback*, 13 February 1995: 8.

8 Sandy Stewart, *From Coast to Coast: A Personal History of Radio in Canada* (Toronto: CBC Enterprises, 1985), 55. See also A.E. Powley, *Broadcasts from the Front: Canadian Radio Overseas in the Second World War* (Toronto: Hakkert, 1975).

9 "TV Graphics: An Important Part of TV Begins on the Drawing Board," CBC *Times*, 16–22 August 1953: 5.

10 See Warner Troyer, *The Sound and the Fury: An Anecdotal History of Broadcasting in Canada* (Toronto: John Wiley and Sons, 1980).

11 A series of documentaries, live reports, and short movies shown on closed circuit television at Montreal's Palais du Commerce.

12 A fifteen-minute compilation of narrated reports, actuality sequences, and dramatized information entitled *Life in Canada*.

13 A story about the Calgary Roundup for the program *Telescope*.

14 See the analysis of *Over Canada* in chapter 5 of this book.

15 Penelope Wise, "On the Air," *Canadian Forum* 17 (October 1952): 158.

16 See Patrick Crawley, "The Canadian Difference in Media," *Cinema Canada* 13, no. 1 (June 1986): 23. Crawley believes documentary television employs a more flexible "Canadian" aesthetic than news programming, which is governed by commercial pressures and "studio authoritarianism." Troyer similarly argues that documentary television is less burdened by restrictions concerning divisions of labour and modes of address and is thus a purer example of Canadian information programming. See Troyer, *The Sound and the Fury*, 154.

17 John Mistaler, "View from Here Cuts Its Edge," *Hot Docs '98 Handbook*: 48. Vision TV's slogan "Real people, real places, real situations, real solutions, really good TV" makes a similar judgment about television.

18 Gail Henley, "For the Record," *Cinema Canada* 14, no. 3 (1985): 17. John Doyle has also declared "too many talking heads" to be the great "curse of the Canadian documentary format." See Doyle,

"Critical List," *Globe and Mail Broadcast Week*, 12 February 2000: 6.

19 Though perhaps partisan because of his position as a documentary producer at the CBC, Mark Starowicz has argued that the genre plays a far more important "citizen-training" role than the nightly news: "No matter how excellent the national newscast," he notes, "it is still a 25 minute bulletin which distills the essence of events and does not conduct debates or discussion ... In order to conduct debates within the paramaters of national priorities [Canadians] require secure and generous electronic information arteries [and] a *documentary capacity*" (emphasis added) (Mark Starowicz, "Citizens of Video America," 94–5).

20 Canada, *Report of the Royal Commission on National Development in the Arts, Letters and Sciences* (Ottawa: King's Printer, 1951): 37, 50–1.

21 Canada, *Report of the Task Force on Broadcast Policy (Caplan-Sauvageau)* (Ottawa: Minister of Supply and Services, 1986): 346–7, 351.

22 Mary Jane Miller, *Turn Up the Contrast: CBC Television Drama since 1952* (Vancouver: University of British Columbia Press and the Canadian Broadcasting Corporation, 1987), 259.

23 Richard Collins, *Culture, Communication and National Identity: The Case of Canadian Television* (Toronto: University of Toronto Press, 1990).

24 Seth Feldman, "The Silent Subject in English Canadian Film," *Canadian Film Studies* 1, no. 1 (June 1984): 17–31.

25 Kevin Dowler, "The Cultural Industries Policy Apparatus," in Michael Dorland, ed., *The Cultural Industries in Canada: Problems, Policies and Prospects* (Toronto: James Lorimer, 1996), 328–46.

26 Wolfe, *Jolts: The TV Wasteland and the Canadian Oasis*, 84.

27 In this sense Canadian documentary television is unique, at least in North America. According to Michael Curtin, for instance, documentary programs have dominated American TV schedules only in rare "overdetermined" moments. He cites the New Frontier era, when the Kennedy administration sought to mobilize popular support for its foreign policies, and the U.S. networks tried to legitimate their overall (entertainment-oriented) operations. See Michael Curtin, *Redeeming the Wasteland: Television Documentary and Cold War Politics* (New Brunswick, N.J.: Rutgers University Press,

1993). By contrast, documentary has been an integral rather than an exceptional genre on Canadian television.

28 For evidence of the globalization of documentary programming in Canada, see chapter 5 of this book and the statistical report commissioned for this study: Statistics Canada: *Tabulations of Documentaries, 1995–97* Catalogue 87F0006XPE/XPF (Ottawa: Minister of Supply and Services, 1998). For recent accounts in the popular press, see Doug Saunders, "Documentary Makers Cast Wary Eye on the Future," *Globe and Mail*, 16 August 1997, C3; and Leo Rice-Barker, "Copros in Canada," *RealScreen* 2, no. 9 (May 1999): 31–46.

29 See, for example, Scott Lash and John Urry, *The End of Organized Capitalism* (Cambridge: Polity Press, 1987); and Scott Lash, *Sociology of Postmodernism* (London: Routledge, 1990).

30 David Harvey, *The Condition of Postmodernity* (Oxford: Blackwell, 1989).

31 See, for example, Edward S. Herman and Robert McChesney, *The Global Media* (London: Cassell, 1997).

32 See, for example, Chris Barker, *Global Television: An Introduction* (Oxford: Blackwell, 1997).

33 See, for example, Ien Ang, *Living Room Wars: Rethinking Media Audiences for a Postmodern World* (London and New York: Routledge, 1996); and Lynn Spigel, "Women's Work," in Horace Newcomb, ed., *Television: The Critical View* (New York: Oxford University Press, 1994).

34 See, for example, Deborah Clarke, "Second Hand News: Production and Reproduction at a Major Ontario Television Station," in Liora Salter, ed., *Communication Studies in Canada* (Toronto: Butterworth, 1980); and Richard V. Ericson, Patricia M. Baranek, and Janet B.L. Chan, *Visualizing Deviance: A Study in News Organization* (Toronto: University of Toronto Press, 1987).

35 Though Grierson did admire some television work, particularly the vérité investigations of producers like Allan King whose *Skid Row* (1956) he arranged to have screened at the 1957 Edinburgh Film Festival. For more on Grierson's understanding of documentary in general and broadcast documentary in particular, see Forsyth Hardy, ed., *Grierson on Documentary* (London: Collins, 1946); Brian Winston, *Claiming the Real*; and John Corner, *The Art of Record: A Critical Introduction to Documentary* (Manchester and New York: Manchester University Press, 1996).

36 Cited in Corner, *The Art of Record*, 66.

37 Gerald Pratley, "NFB," *Canadian Forum* 46, no. 3 (August 1956): 110–11.

38 Peter Steven, *Brink of Reality: New Canadian Documentary Film and Video* (Toronto: Between the Lines, 1992).

39 Ibid., 173.

40 Magnus Isaacson, "The Fate of Documentary in a Television Age," *Cinema Canada* 123 (October 1985): 21.

41 See, for example, Paula Rabinowicz, *They Must Be Represented: The Politics of Documentary* (London: Verso, 1994).

42 See, for example, Seth Feldman, "The Silent Subject in English Canadian Film": 17–31.

43 See, for example, Nancy Shaw, "Cultural Democracy and Institutionalized Difference," in Janine Marchessault, ed., *Mirror Machine: Video and Identity* (Toronto: YYZ, 1995): 26–34.

44 Winston, *Claiming the Real*, 172.

45 Janine Marchessault, "Amateur Video and the Challenge for Change," in Marchessault, ed., *Mirror Machine: Video and Identity*, 13–25. Of course, the NFB did shake off the aesthetic influence of Grierson in the 1950s, but we should keep in mind Druick's observation that most NFB films were "unexceptional and unmemorable" in television's first decade (the focus of chapter 3 of this book) with "few filmmakers able to bend the government film objectives enough to create works of art" (Zoe Druick, "Documenting Government: Reexamining the National Film Board Films about Citizenship," *Canadian Journal of Film Studies* 9, no. 1 [spring 2000]: 3–4).

46 Magnus Isaacson, "What Is to Be Done?: Crisis in Documentary," *Cinema Canada* 158 (December 1988): 12.

47 Perhaps an observation will help illustrate. Documentary television's preoccupation with everyday, practical matters is often cited as proof of its inherent conservatism – that is, its refusal to critically examine the larger political and social arrangements of its time. But in Canada one could argue that this "current affairs" bias has actually helped draw attention to the political nature of *day-to-day* issues, thereby breaking down gendered distinctions between public and private affairs (see chapter 4, concerning vérité television). In other words, far from blunting its political edge, this concern with "everyday" matters may have been the source of documentary television's disruptive power.

48 John Corner and Kay Richardson, "Documentary Meanings and the Discourse of Interpretation," in John Corner, ed., *Documentary and the Mass Media* (London: Edward Arnold, 1986), 141–53.

49 "Alternative" documentary films in Canada, for instance, were beginning to stress the reality and indexical authority of their images just as "mainstream" television documentaries in the United States were beginning to employ increasingly non-realist forms of symbolic montage in the early 1970s. See Marchessault, "Amateur Video"; and Richard Schaeffer, "Editing Strategies in Television News Documentaries," *Journal of Communication* 47, no. 4 (1997): 69–88. Some television researchers share the film studies prejudice. According to John Fiske, documentary programming frequently denies viewers "popular pleasures" by preventing them from "reading into the text." See Fiske, "Popular News," in *Reading the Popular* (Boston: Unwin Hyman, 1989): 185–98.

50 See John Ellis, *Visible Fictions* (London: Routledge 1982); and John Caughie, "Playing at Being American," in Patricia Mellencamp, ed., *Logics of Television: Essays in Cultural Criticism* (Bloomington: Indiana University Press, 1990).

51 Corner and Richardson, "Documentary Meanings," 149.

52 John Corner, *Television Form and Public Address* (London: Edward Arnold, 1995), 86.

53 Mary Ross. "Television," *Saturday Night* (16 April 1965): 24.

54 Jeremy Tunstall, *Television Producers* (New York: Routledge, 1993).

55 Magnus Isaacson, "Documentary Out in the Cold," *Cinema Canada* 158 (December 1988): 12.

56 Canadian Independent Film Caucus, Letter to Communications Minister Francis Fox, undated, 1983.

57 See, for example, Seth Feldman, "Docudrama since the 'Tar Sands,'" *Cinema Canada* 142 (June 1987): 16.

58 See David J. Bercuson and S.F. Wise, eds., *The Valour and the Horror Revisited* (Montreal and Kingston: McGill-Queen's University Press, 1994); and David Taras, "Struggles over the Valour and the Horror: Media Power and the Portrayal of War," *Canadian Journal of Political Science* 28, no. 4 (1995): 417–35.

59 See CTV, *Policy and Style Handbook* (Toronto: CTV, 1993), 10, 21; and CBC, *Journalistic Policy* (Toronto: CBC, 1991).

60 *Canadian Television Fund Documentary Module 1999–2000* (Canadian Television Fund: 1999): 1.

61 See Steve Neale, "Questions of Genre," *Screen* 33, no. 1 (Spring 1990): 44–66.

62 Doug Saunders. "Uneven Immigration Rules Keep Canadian Film Crews out of U.S.," *Globe and Mail*, 26 June 1999: A10.

63 Charles Jennings, CBC director of programming, internal memo, 29 April 1954, CBC National Archives Papers, RG41, Series A-V-2/ vol. 893/PG8-1-1, Public Affairs Programming General Correspondence, 1939–61.

64 Wolfe, *Jolts*, 78.

65 See, for example, Knowlton Nash, *Prime Time at Ten* (Toronto: McClelland and Stewart, 1987), 81.

66 Documentary fashions have changed dramatically amongst academics as well. In 1962 one film theorist dubbed hosted magazine shows television's "one distinctive contribution ... to the [documentary] form." Five years earlier a communications professor at the University of British Columbia had argued that docudramas would one day make traditional documentaries "obsolete." See Benjamin Burton, "The Documentary Heritage," *Television Quarterly* 7, no. 1 (February 1962): 29–34; and Alan Thomas, "On Television," *Food for Thought* (September–October 1957): 206. Both forms have long since gone out of fashion in academic circles.

67 See Lawrence Grossberg, Introduction: "Re-Placing the Popular," in *Dancing in Spite of Myself* (Durham, N.C.: Duke University Press 1997), 1–26.

68 Donna Lypchuk, "Ou sont les documentaires d'antan," *Cinema Canada* 157 (October 1989): 27. See also Robert Fulford's judgment that CTV documentary programs "amounted to very little" twenty-five years earlier, in Robert Fulford, "What's Behind the New Wave of TV Think Shows," *Maclean's* (5 October 1963): 25.

69 See Richard Collins's argument to this effect in his *Culture, Communication and National Identity: The Case of Canadian Television*, 208–10. Recent data supplied by Statscan similarly suggest that documentary programs are less watched in Quebec than in English Canada. See Statistics Canada, *Tabulations of Documentaries*, 1995–97, especially p. 3 regarding French-language viewing patterns.

70 Seth Feldman. "The Electronic Fable: Aspects of the Docudrama in Canada," *Canadian Drama* 8 (1983): 41.

71 See, for example, Gary Evans, *In the National Interest: A Chronicle of the National Film Board from 1949 to 1989* (Toronto:

University of Toronto Press, 1991); and Joyce Nelson, *The Colonized Eye: Rethinking the Griersonian Legend* (Toronto: Between the Lines, 1988).

CHAPTER TWO

1 Bernard Trotter, supervisor public affairs, Toronto, to J.D. Nixon, director of programming (English), 24 January 1961; "The NFB," CBC National Archives Papers, RG 41/series A-V-2/vol. 893/file no. PG8-3, pt. 1: Public Affairs Program Reports 1954–79.
2 Ted Magder, *Canada's Hollywood: The Canadian State and Feature Films* (Toronto: University of Toronto Press, 1993), 3.
3 National Film Act, section 9 (a), cited in Canada: *Report of the Royal Commission on National Development in the Arts, Letters and Sciences (Massey-Levesque)* (Ottawa: King's Printer, 1951), 51.
4 Peter Morris, "Backwards to the Future: John Grierson's Film Policy for Canada," in *Flashback: People and Institutions in Canadian Film History* (Montreal: Mediatexte, 1986), 17–35.
5 John Grierson, cited in Raymond Fielding, *The March of Time, 1935–51* (New York: Oxford University Press, 1978), 6.
6 Evans, *In the National Interest*, 7–11.
7 Cited in Winston, *Claiming the Real*, 60.
8 Morris, "Backwards to the Future."
9 Nelson, *The Colonized Eye*.
10 Feldman, "The Silent Subject in English Canadian Film."
11 Winston, *Claiming the Real*, 37.
12 Ibid.; and John Corner, *The Art of Record: A Critical Introduction to Documentary* (Manchester and New York: Manchester University Press, 1996), 12. The NFB shook off the aesthetic influence of Grierson in the 1950s, but that is not the period I am concerned with here. As Zoe Druick has observed, most NFB films were "unexceptional and unmemorable" in television's first decade (the focus of chapter 3 of this book) with "few filmmakers able to bend the government film objectives enough to create works of art." See Zoe Druick, "Documenting Government: Reexamining The National Film Board Films about Citizenship": 3–4.
13 *Massey Report*, 53.
14 Feldman, "The Electronic Fable," 41.
15 "What's On," CBC *Times* (9–15 March 1953): 4.

16 CRBC, *Annual Report* (1935–36): 13.

17 For a comparison of radio and cinema modes of production at the time, see Harry Boyle, CBC National Conference Outside Broadcasts Department, 27 November–1 December 1961, Appendix B, CBC National Archives Papers, RG 41, series A-V-2, vol. 851, PG1-13, pt. 3.

18 Ibid.

19 Magazine documentaries had been featured on American radio since at least 1934, pioneered in large part by public affairs producer Mary Margaret McBride. See Michele Hilmes, "Desired and Feared: Women's Voices in Radio History," in Mary Beth Haralovich and Lauren Rabinovitz, eds., *Television, History and American Culture* (Durham and London: Duke University Press, 1999), 30.

20 "Saturday Magazine," CBC *Times* (17–23 April 1949): 5.

21 Boyle, Appendix B, 5.

22 Ibid.

23 A.E. Powley, *Broadcast from the Front: Canadian Radio Overseas in the Second World War* (Toronto: Hakkert, 1975), x.

24 Boyle, Appendix B, 12.

25 Frank Peers, "Talks and Public Affairs," *Radio* 14, no. 4 (April 1958): 7.

26 Ibid.

27 Ibid.

28 Boyle, Appendix B, 18–19; See also Trotter, "The NFB."

29 CBC *Annual Report* (1945–46): 21.

30 "Armed Forces in Peacetime," CBC *Times* (22–28 July 1948): 5.

31 "Listeners Eavesdrop on a Family Trailer Trip in the West," CBC *Times* (30 July – 5 August 1948): 3.

32 "Cross Section," CBC *Times* (21–27 October 1951): 5.

33 Boyle, Appendix B, 12.

34 Powley, *Broadcast from the Front*, 56–7.

35 Ibid., 56.

36 R.S. Bryden, "Atlantic Odyssey II," CBC *Times* (5–11 January 1958): 3.

37 Bryden, "Atlantic Odyssey I," CBC *Times* (22–28 December 1957): 5.

38 Powley, *Broadcast from the Front*, x.

39 Ibid., 15.

40 "Small Town," CBC *Times* (17–24 August 1951): 5. Most producers assumed Canadian audiences loved this sort of "low key

realism." Docudrama producer Frank Willis insisted listeners would want to "relive the humdrum dialogue and [identify] every sound" of the average Canadian home. Quoted in Bryden, "Atlantic Odyssey II," 3.

41 Powley, *Broadcast from the Front*, 17.

42 Sandy Stewart, *From Coast to Coast: A Personal History of Radio in Canada*, 55. As Stewart notes, these sounds were in turn used by the BBC and other broadcasters who considered them the best on record.

43 Troyer, *The Sound and the Fury*, 150–2.

44 Murrow's famous coverage of the London Blitz, for instance, consisted entirely of live and unedited reports. Other American radio shows offered few if any location recordings during the war. By contrast, virtually all the CBC's war coverage on location consisted of documentary reports, with only one brief wartime dispatch broadcast live and unedited to Canada (from Rome in 1943 when the U.S. Army allowed reporter Peter Stursberg to use its high-powered radio transmitters.)

45 Boyle, Appendix B, 16.

46 "Cross Section," CBC *Times* (25–31 May 1952): 5.

47 Troyer, *The Sound and the Fury*, 77.

48 "In Rehearsal: A Wednesday Night Docudrama," CBC *Times* (28 February – 6 March 1954): 5.

49 R.S. Bryden, "Atlantic Odyssey I," CBC *Times* (22–28 December 1957): 5.

50 "In Rehearsal," 5.

51 A discourse more fully developed in Canada than in the United States, where union rules required that effects be produced live and in the studio without any location recording. Broadcast documentary's eclectic combination of live, recorded, and rigged sounds in Canada was thus quite unique in the world of North American radio.

52 See National Archives of Canada, *Beyond the Printed Word: Newsreel and Broadcast Reporting in Canada* (Ottawa: Supply and Services Canada, 1988). Newsreels were imported from American sources such as Hearst, Pathe, and Universal as early as 1897. Canada's own Associated Screen News made films from 1920 to 1952. Though the form was often dismissed by broadcasters and filmmakers as alien and artless, many CBC and NFB producers received their formative training with these shows. Sidney

Newman and Ross McLean, to name just two, worked for the American newsreel program *March of Time*.

53 Listed as "one of the most popular types of program" of the early public service schedule in CRBC, *Annual Report* (1935–36): 13.

54 The program began with a bet by writer Don Henshaw that he could use reenactments to bring the museum's history to life.

55 "Mokatum," CBC *Times* (22–28 July 1951): 5.

56 "Cross Section," CBC *Times* (17–23 October 1954): 5.

57 Mavis Gallant, "Culture on the Air," *Winnipeg Standard* (8 October 1949): 8.

58 Paul Rutherford, *The Making of the Canadian Media* (Toronto: McGraw-Hill Ryerson, 1978).

59 Ibid., 86.

60 Troyer, *The Sound and the Fury*, 150–2.

61 Powley, *Broadcast from the Front*, 133.

62 Cited in ibid., 99.

63 Ibid., 133–4.

64 CBC, *Annual Report* (1941–42): 9.

65 CBC, *Annual Report* (1944–45): 9.

66 Powley, *Broadcast from the Front*, 107.

67 CBC, *Annual Report* (1943–44): 9.

68 Boyle, Appendix B, 14.

69 CBC, *Annual Report* (1938–39): 9.

70 CBC, *Annual Report* (1940–41): 9.

71 CBC *Annual Report* (1940–41): 9.

72 "Log Drive: 1953," CBC *Times* (17–23 July 1953): 2.

73 "Small Town," CBC *Times* (17–23 August 1953): 7.

74 "Yellowknife Report," CBC *Times* (23–29 July 1948): 5.

75 "Canadian Scene," CBC *Times* (3–9 October 1954): 11.

76 Hunter C. Lewis. "Mokatum: Preface to the Broadcast," CBC *Times* (2–8 September 1951): 7.

77 Ibid.

78 "The Indian Way," CBC *Times* (2–8 July 1951): 7.

79 "This Week," CBC *Times* (9–15 December 1951): 11.

80 "CBC Programs for Women," CBC *Times* (18–24 June 1950): 2.

81 "Women in Business, CBC *Times* (4–11 August 1948): 2.

82 Though perhaps less so than their U.S. counterparts. For an account of the way women were subordinated by the institutional and discursive practices of American radio, see Michele Hilmes, "Desired and Feared: Women's Voices in Radio History," in Mary

Beth Haralovich and Lauren Rabinovitz, eds., *Television History and American Culture* (Durham: Duke University Press, 1996), 17–35.

83 One could further argue that the programs were an exercise in "governmentality" in the Foucauldian sense, given their relentless preoccupation with "difference," and their steadfast assertion of a public interest in private life. In this way, the programs may have worked to produce functional loyal citizens in line with the security objectives of the postwar nation-state. But again, the same can be said of documentary films, as Druick has persuasively argued. See Druick, "Documenting Government."

84 Boyle, Appendix B, 14.

85 Canadians, like subjects around the world, took slowly to the informal banter required by new broadcast forms. For his special 1940 feature *The Leslie Howards at Home*, producer Rob Bowman resorted to airing a rehearsal rather than an interview itself, because even this "trained communicator of film and stage" was apparently unused to more informal types of exchange. See Powley, *Broadcast from the Front*, 17. Broadcast documentary thus trained a new generation of subjects for public discourse.

86 CBC *Annual Report* (1942–43): 7.

87 "In Search of Ourselves," CBC *Times* (7–13 November 1954): 6.

88 For a similar argument from a non-Canadian source, see Winston, *Claiming the Real*, 46.

89 NFB, *Brief to the Massey Commision* (RG 33, 28, vol. 9, nos. 102–7a): 62.

90 Ibid., 63.

91 Ibid.

92 CBC, *Brief to the Massey Commision* (RG 33, 28, vol. 9, nos. 102–7a): 36.

93 Ibid.: 37.

CHAPTER THREE

1 Mavor Moore, "What We'll Do with TV," *Saturday Night* (24 May 1952): 4–6.

2 Ibid.

3 *Massey-Levesque Report*, 50–1

4 Ibid., 51.

5 Ibid., 40–1.

6 Ibid., 38.
7 See Paul Litt, *The Muses, the Masses and the Massey Commission* (Toronto: University of Toronto Press, 1992).
8 *Massey-Levesque Report*, 296.
9 Ibid., 297.
10 Ibid., 311.
11 The commission advised the CBC to make use of a "proper proportion" of NFB films and employ the Film Board as a "principal advisor on film matters" (304).
12 Ibid., 296.
13 The report noted that discussion groups had partly corrected the passive viewing habits associated with ordinary broadcasting (pp. 37–38). Listener groups were a staple of radio forum and discussion programs, and had been used for documentary series such as *In Search of Ourselves*.
14 "Life in Canada Today," CBC *Times* (14–20 March 1954): 3.
15 Fred Rainsberry, "Is Television Bad for Children?" CBC *Times*, (17–23 March 1957): 3.
16 Gallant, "Culture on the Air," *Winnipeg Standard* (8 October 1949).
17 S.O. Wilson, CBC Internal Memo, "TV Programs on Film," undated, CBC National Archives Papers, RG41/series A. II.1/ vol. 990/file 19/pt. 1; TV Memoranda 1948–50.
18 Liss Jeffrey, "Private Television and Cable," in Michael Dorland, ed., *The Cultural Industries in Canada: Problems, Policies and Prospects* (Toronto: James Lorimer, 1996), 203–56.
19 Letter from A.D. Dunton, Chairman, CBC, to Lord Beveridge, chairman, British Broadcasting Corporation (26 April 1950): 2, (CBC National Archives Papers; RG41/series A.II.1/vol. 988/ file 2/pt. 1; Correspondence with BBC 1946–56. Dunton noted that the CBC was "not primarily interested in competition with private stations" in the information programming area, but went on to admit that "like any broadcasting organization [we are] interested in estimates of the number of people tuned in ... and this inevitably puts pressure on thinking and planning here." That pressure appears to have been cumulative. In 1954 CBC audience surveys were not even distributed to many producers in the Talks and Public Affairs department because of "doubts about their accuracy" (CBC National Program Office, Minutes, 5–6 January 1954, CBC National Archives Papers, RG41/Series A-V-2, vol. 851/PGI-13/ pt. 2, National Progam Office Meetings 1953–57). By the end of

the decade audience panel reports appear to have been consulted by virtually all public affairs producers, even if their significance was sometimes dismissed. At magazine shows such as *Tabloid* and *Close-Up* the selection of items was always "affected by the potential appeal for a general audience" (Frank Peers, CBC Internal Memo, 7 August 1957, CBC National Archives Papers, RG41–27, Talks and Public Affairs Archives, Box 77).

20 CBC National Program Office, Minutes (17–18 November 1953): 1.

21 Felix Jackson, "Television and Its Rivals in the Living Room," *CBC Times* (5–12 December 1953): 11.

22 "Junior Magazine," *CBC Times* (9–15 September 1956): 3.

23 Alan Sangster, "On the Air," *Canadian Forum* (February 1954): 254.

24 Gilbert Seldes, *Writing for Television* (New York: Doubleday, 1952), 183.

25 Ibid., 184.

26 Ibid.

27 Ibid., 189, 191.

28 Ibid., 190.

29 Ibid., 192.

30 Ibid., 193.

31 Ibid., 189.

32 Ibid., 191.

33 Ibid., 188–9.

34 CBC National Program Office, Minutes (17–18 November 1953).

35 Eugene Hallman, supervising producer, Talks and Public Affairs, "Documentary Series," CBC Internal Memo, 9 December 1955, CBC National Archives Papers, RG41/series A-V-2/vol. 895/PG8-3/pt. 1: Public Affairs Program Reports.

36 Ibid.

37 Ibid.

38 Eugene Hallman, supervising producer, Talks and Public Affairs, CBC Internal Memo, 6 December 1955, "Life Magazine on the Air," CBC National Archives Papers, RG41/series A-V-2/vol. 895/PG8-3/pt. 1: Public Affairs Program Reports.

39 Harry Rassky, "Harry Rassky Says: You Meet So Many Interesting People," *CBC Times* (23–29 August 1953): 5.

40 "Explorations," *CBC Times* (24–30 November 1957): 12.

41 "Scope," *CBC Times* (19–25 December 1954): 3.

42 Hallman, "Documentary Series," 5.

43 "Graphic," CBC *Times* (February 26–March 3 1956): 3.

44 "CBC Newsmagazine," CBC *Times* (23–29 August 1954): 5. In its first two years on the air, *Newsmagazine* shot over 400 miles of film, less than 5 per cent of which was actually shown. Some of the outtakes were used for newscasts and other public affairs shows. See "CBC Newsmagazine," CBC *Times* (10–16 October 1954): 2.

45 Frank Peers, director, Talks and Public Affairs, to Charles Jennings, director of Programming, CBC Internal Memo, 29 January 1954, CBC National Archives Papers, RG41/series A-V-2/PG81-1-1/pt. 1: Public Affairs Programs – General Correspondence 1939–61.

46 Frank Peers to Robert Patchell, Talks and Public Affairs producer, CBC Internal Memo, 20 December 1956 (CBC National Archives Papers, RG41/series A-V-2/vol. 895/PG8-3/pt. 1: Public Affairs Program Reports.

47 Charles Jennings to Frank Peers, CBC Internal Memo, 29 April 1954, CBC National Archives Papers, RG41/series A-V-2/PG81-1-1/pt. 1: Public Affairs Programs – General Correspondence 1939–61.

48 CBC National Program Office, Minutes, 23–24 November 1954, 9. Early plans for the NFB to provide more television documentaries bogged down even before the new service went on the air, partly because of the costs involved and partly because of disagreements over editorial control. The CBC never trusted the Film Board's "partisan and subjective style" (10).

49 Hallman, "Life Magazine on the Air," 2. As the CBC moved away from TV discussion shows in the late 1950s, the influence of educators over programming waned. Producers insisted that new documentary formats could not be "made by committee" (W.H. Hogg, director of News and Public Affairs to H.G. Walker, general manager [English network], CBC Internal Memo, 2 June 1965, CBC National Archive Papers, RG41/series A-V-2/vol. 852/PG1-18-1-2, pt. 1, Program Archives – Administration 1958–74.

50 "Graphic," CBC *Times* (26 February–3 March 1953): 1.

51 "Perspective," CBC *Times* (1–7 April 1956): 2.

52 "The Thread of Life," CBC *Times* (26 November–2 December 2): 13.

53 "Explorations," CBC *Times* (24–30 November 1957): 12.

54 "Graphic," CBC *Times* (26 February–3 March 1953): 1.

55 "Television: Country Style," *Radio* (July–August 1956): 7.

56 Mary Ross, "Riding the Microwaves," *Saturday Night* (2 August 1958): 2. Most CBC producers agreed. The CBC's 1961 National Conference of the Outside Broadcasts Department, for instance, concluded that "in documentary we can secure a whole variety of people from all corners of the earth and then compile an astounding and authoritative show ... Money couldn't buy the landlines needed to gather this material." See CBC National Conference Outside Broadcasts Department, 27 November – 1 December 1961, CBC National Archives Papers, RG 41, series A-V-2, vol. 851, PG1-13, pt. 3: 23.

57 TV, as one producer put it, "jazzed up the form." See "Facts with Fun: Ross McLean's Motto for 'Tabloid,'" CBC *Times* (24–30 January 1954): 3.

58 "Graphic," CBC *Times* (26 February–3 March 1956): 5.

59 Eric Koch, *Inside Seven Days* (Scarborough: Prentice-Hall Canada, 1991), 14–20.

60 Video was introduced to network and regional offices as early as 1956. The CBC insisted it offered a "more faithful reproduction of picture and sound." See "Pacific 13," CBC *Times* (11–17 November 1956): 6.

61 Video was the basis for "immediate, flexible and visually acute reports," the corporation claimed in 1964. See "On the Scene," CBC *Times* (10–16 October 1964): 8.

62 This was a very different job from movie scoring. At the NFB Applebaum was usually given at least two weeks to write a piece of film music. At the CBC he was often given two days, sometimes scoring a program he hadn't even seen. See "Louis Applebaum: TV Composer," CBC *Times* (11–17 March 1957): 5.

63 Fred Kruper, "An Important Part of TV Begins on the Drawing Board," CBC *Times* (16–22 August 1956): 5.

64 Ibid.

65 "Facts with Fun: Ross McLean's Motto for 'Tabloid'": 3.

66 Ibid.

67 Ibid.

68 CBC National Program Office, Minutes (2–4 March 1955): 3.

69 Frank Rassky, "CBC Flirts with Sponsors," *Saturday Night* (14 September 1957): 7.

70 CBC Public Affairs editor Jo Kowin, for instance, noted the Film Unit's reluctance to take part in productions combining live broadcasts and recorded film. See Jo Kowin, "Explorations,"

CBC Internal Memo, 26 August 1956: 2, CBC National Archives Papers, RG41/series A-V-2/vol. 895/PG1-1, pt. 1: Programming – General Correspondence 1952–74.

71 Ibid.

72 Marion Lepkin, "Speaking of Television," *Winnipeg Free Press*, 4 August 1956.

73 Ron Poulton, "A Mirror for Canada," *Toronto Telegram*, 25 October 1956.

74 "Graphic," CBC *Times* (26 February–3 March 1956): 3.

75 "CBC Newsmagazine," CBC *Times* (12–18 February 1956): 6.

76 "Speak Your Mind," CBC *Times* (16–22 December 1956): 9.

77 "Skid Row," CBC *Times* (13–19 January 1957): 5.

78 "Candid Eye," CBC *Times* (26 October–1 November 1958): 3.

79 "Skid Row": 5.

80 "Candid Eye," CBC *Times* (28 September–4 October 1958): 14.

81 Kowin, "Explorations," 3 (emphasis in the original).

82 CBC, *Annual Report* (1936–37): 11.

83 CBC, *Annual Report* (1939–40): 14.

84 "CBC Newsmagazine," CBC *Times* (21–27 July 1957): 5.

85 Hallman, "Life Magazine on the Air," 3.

86 Ibid.

87 Hugh Gillis, "Talks and Public Affairs," *Radio* (April 1958): 9.

88 "CBC Newsmagazine," CBC *Times* (21–27 July 1957): 5.

89 J. Brehl, "McLean Gets Plum Job," *Toronto Daily Star*, 22 June 1957.

90 Ibid.

91 "CBC Tabloid," CBC *Times* (21–27 July 1957): 6.

92 *Newsmagazine*'s Harry Rassky recalled producing two stories about a political meeting and a beauty contest in the space of an hour. In such circumstances "encounter" stories were all that time allowed. See "CBC Newsmagazine," CBC *Times* (23–29 August 1953): 5.

93 Ibid.

94 Hugh Garner, "Ad Lib, News and Tabloid," *Saturday Night* (19 January 1954): 13. Saltzman also took to wearing fake eyeglasses to appear more "learned."

95 "CBC Newsmagazine," CBC *Times* (23–29 August 1953): 5.

96 "New Programs," CBC *Times* (31 August–5 September 1958): 6.

97 Ibid.

98 Garner, "Ad Lib, News and Tabloid," 13.

99 Ibid. The onus was on hosts to make sense of their material because location footage was often unavailable or incoherent. The Hart House "footage," for instance, came from a single camera trained on a swimming pool. Early documentary programs thus relied heavily on spoken as opposed to enacted narratives. Concerning infomation television's reliance on these forms, see John Corner, *Critical Ideas in Television Studies* (Oxford: Clarendon, 1999), 53.

100 In the early 1960s many French network public affairs hosts conducted research, wrote scripts, and even helped edit film (see, for instance, Jean-Guy Pilon, "Animateurs," CBC Internal Memo, 29 July 1963: 11, CBC National Archive Papers, RG41/series A-V-2/vol. 852/PG1-18-1-2, pt. 1, Program Archives – Administration 1958–74). These activities were generally curtailed as newsroom divisions of labour became more fixed (see chapter 4).

101 CBC National Program Office Meeting, Minutes (2–3 February 1954): 4.

102 CBC National Program Office Meeting, Minutes 7–8 December 1953): 7.

103 Ibid.

104 CBC National Program Office Meeting, Minutes (17–18 November 1953): 9–10.

105 CBC National Program Office Meeting, Minutes (9–10 September 1954): 8.

106 CBC National Program Office Meeting, Minutes (23–24 November 1954): 7.

107 CBC National Program Office Meeting, Minutes (7–8 April 1954): 8.

108 D.C. MacArthur, CBC Internal Memo, 6 January 1964: 1, CBC National Archives Papers, RG41/series A-V-2/vol. 849, PG1-7, pt. 2, Programming: General Joint Program Planning Group 1963–65.

109 "How to Be an Interviewer," CBC *Times* (14–20 November 1959): 7.

110 110) Harold Walker, "Inquiry," CBC Internal Memo, 14 May 1964: 1, CBC National Archives Papers, RG41/series A-V-2/ vol. 849, PG1-7, pt. 2, "Programming: General Joint Program Planing Group 1963–65.

111 Robert Fulford, "What's Behind the New Wave of TV Think Shows," *Maclean's* (5 October 1963): 24–6.

112 Ibid.

113 Nathan Cohen, "Time for a Change at the CBC," *Toronto Star,*
     14 September 1963.
114 Ibid.
115 Though still somewhat smaller than those for American entertain-
     ment shows such as *Bonanza* and *The Ed Sullivan Show* (ibid,
     31).
116 Henry Stephens, "Seven Days and Seven Lessons," *Toronto Daily
     Star,* 4 January 1966.
117 Ibid.
118 Ibid.
119 *Document,* for instance, was castigated for supposedly staging a
     drug orgy for a 1966 program entitled "Youth and Morality"
     (a charge the producers vigorously denied). See R.C. Fraser, vice-
     president, to Christina MacDougall, program organizer, Public
     Affairs, CBC Internal Memo, 1 May 1967, CBC National Archives
     Papers, RG41/series A-V-2/vol. 849, PG1-7, pt. 3, Programming:
     General Joint Program Planing Group 1965–70.
120 Shirley Marr, "Showdown in the CBC Corral," *Maclean's*
     (5 November 1961): 80.
121 Bob Blackburn, "CBC's 'Close Up' Strikes Out," 4 October 1958,
     Ottawa Citizen. Blackburn suspected a "hidden agenda on the part
     of the show's producers," despite McLean's earlier assurances that
     while he liked jazz and theatre, he still "dated girls" (J.D. Brehl,
     "McLean Get Plum Job").
122 Kenneth Caple, director of public affairs, British Columbia, to
     H.G. Walker, general manager (English network), CBC Internal
     Memo, 29 November 1966, CBC Public Archives Papers, RG41,
     Series A-V-2, vol. 897, PG8, pt. 1, Public Affairs Programs: The
     Sixties, 1964–66.
123 J.P. Gilmore, vice president, Planning, CBC Internal Memo, 13 Feb-
     ruary 1967, CBC Public Archives Papers, RG41, series A-V-2,
     vol. 897, PG8, pt. 1, Public Affairs Programs: The Sixties, 1964–
     66. A later supervisor was similarly appalled by the "permissive-
     ness built into" a 1970 *Tuesday Night* story on homosexuality.
     Particularly galling was the "graphic depiction of normal and
     abnormal physical love." See M.L. Munro, assistant general man-
     ager, to Norn Garriock, managing director, Television (English),
     CBC Internal Memo, 23 December 1970, CBC National Archive
     Papers, RG41/Series A-V-2/vol. 852/PG1-18-1-2, pt. 1, Program
     Archives – Administration 1958–74.

124 Peter Johnson, "How Lively the Arts?" *Winnipeg Free Press*, 16 October 1961.

125 "The Nature of Things," CBC *Times* (17–23 December 1960): 7.

126 Johnson, "How Lively the Arts."

127 Harold Wright, "For Better Cutting on Television," *Radio* (January 1954): 16–17.

128 Harold Wright, "Technical Aspects of TV Production," *Radio* (March 1954): 16.

129 Fred Kruper, "An Important Part of TV ..."

130 Pierre Normandin, "Le Bruitage," *Radio* (December 1956): 10.

131 "Louis Applebaum: TV Composer," CBC *Times* (11–17 March 1957): 5.

132 Marion Lepkin, "Speaking of Television," *Winnipeg Free Press*, 4 August 1956.

133 Seldes, *Writing for Television*, 196.

134 Miriam Waddington, "Radio and TV," *Canadian Forum* (July 1956): 234.

135 Harold Wright, "For Better Cutting," 17.

136 CBC National Program Office Meeting, Minutes (17–18 November 1953): 7–8.

137 Koch, *Inside Seven Days*, 83.

138 Stephens, "Seven Days and Seven Lessons."

139 Steven Rosco, "CBC Public Affairs Gets a Boost," *Toronto Telegram*, 5 February 1963.

140 Stephens, "Seven Days and Seven Lessons." See also Koch, *Inside Seven Days*: 69.

141 Harry Rassky, "Harry Rassky Says: You Meet So Many Interesting People," CBC *Times* (23–29 August 1953): 5.

142 Stephens, "Seven Days and Seven Lessons."

143 Allan Sangster, "On the Air," *Canadian Forum* (October 1954): 200.

144 Hugh Gillis, "Talks and Public Affairs," *Radio* (April 1958): 9. According to CBC supervisor Doddi Robb, only daytime current affairs producers believed women were "intelligent and lively and curious people who like to think and learn and know." See "Take 30," CBC *Times* (18–24 September 1965): 10.

145 CBC, *Annual Report* (1954–55): 13.

146 CBC, *Annual Report* (1956–57): 21.

147 "New 'Take 30' Shows," CBC *Times* (24–30 September 1966): 13.

148 Kowin was prevented from developing her "non-institutional" approach because of resistance from the CBC Film Unit (Jo

Kowin, editor, Talks and Public Affairs, to Eugene Hallman, supervising producer, Talks and Public Affairs, CBC Internal Memo, 26 August 1956, CBC National Archives Papers, RG41/ series A-V-2/vol. 895/PG1-1, pt. 1; Programming: General Correspondence 1952–74.

149 "Open House Wins Ohio Award," CBC *Times* (13–19 May 1961): 31.

150 Allan Sangster, "On the Air," *Canadian Forum* (January 1953): 231.

151 Ibid.

152 Steven Singer, "Women's Work Is Never Done," *Saturday Night* (21 November 1953): 10.

153 "Explorations," CBC *Times* (21–27 October 1956): 3.

154 Ibid.

155 Interview with Vincent Tovell, 18 April 1997: 7.

156 Felix Lazarus, CBC Winnipeg, CBC Internal Memo, 12 October 1958, CBC National Archives Papers, RG41/series A-V-2/vol. 895/ PG1-1, pt. 1; Programming: General Correspondence 1952–74.

157 *Massey-Levesque Report,* 311.

158 Lyn Spigel, "High Culture in Low Places," in Cary Nelson and D.P. Gaonkar, eds., *Disciplinarity and Dissent in Cultural Studies* (New York and London: Routledge, 1996), 313–46.

159 See, for instance, Ien Ang, *Living Room Wars: Rethinking Media Audiences for a Postmodern World* (London and New York: Routledge, 1996).

CHAPTER FOUR

1 See Corner, *The Art of Record*; and Winston, *Claiming the Real*.

2 "Hipdom's Homeland," CBC *Times* (23–29 March 1967): 3.

3 "The Way It Is," CBC *Times* (23–29 September 1967): 3.

4 This program, about the human cost of unemployment, led to an intense debate about whether real tears should be shown on television, and at what price. Some network officials considered genuine displays of emotion to be properly private, while critics charged that emotion was fake if expressed in the course of a paid interview – as was the case in King's piece. See Allan King, "Ironic Ethics," *Cinema Canada* 102 (December 1983): 23.

5 "National Survival," CBC *Times* (7–13 November 1959): 7. Reporters Ross and Kay Parry volunteered for the experiment,

spending 168 hours below ground to demonstrate the psychological effects of life in a bomb shelter. The CBC claimed that this was one of its most popular specials ever, and the couple were reportedly greeted by hundreds of fans when they emerged.

6 Winston, *Claiming the Real*, 187.

7 Stanley Kauffman, "Children of Our Time," *The Nation*, 21 September 1968.

8 R.C. Fraser, vice-president, assistant to the president, "Hidden Microphones and Cameras," CBC Internal Memo, 1 May 1967, CBC National Public Archives Papers, RG41, series A. 11.1/vol. 851/ PG1-14, pt. 1, Prevention of Unethical Program Practices, 1959–67.

9 See Gilbert Seldes, "Reporter? Peeping Tom? The TV Camera," *Saturday Night* 4 (December 1954): 12–15.

10 Pearson developed his own camera smarts when some of his unguarded remarks were recorded for Richard Ballantyne's early TV vérité piece, *Mr Peason*. Pearson's handlers helped hold up the final cut, which was not aired until 1969 (Koch, *Inside Seven Days*, 21).

11 "Document's 'Servant of All: Anatomy of an Election,'" CBC *Times* (15–21 September 1962): 11–12.

12 "Manipulating Images for TV," CBC *Times* (1–9 March 1969): 10–11.

13 Christopher Harris, "Warrendale: Still Harrowing after 30 Years," *Globe and Mail*, 22 January 1997: C1.

14 Koch, *Inside Seven Days*, 21. Many critics also had problems with the sound of vérité. For instance, William Drylie complained that a 1957 *Close-Up* portrait of Paul Anka was unintelligible because of the "mumblings" of the singer and his fans. See William Drylie, "Anka Show Misses Mark," *Toronto Daily Star*, 25 November 1957. Similar complaints were made about later shows due to the lack of "close-miking" technology at the time. Some sound and image problems were resolved as videotape units came into use in the late 1960s.

15 Alan Rosenthal, *The New Documentary in Action: A Casebook in Filmmaking* (Berkeley: University of California Press, 1971).

16 Allan King, cited in "Allan King: Lifetime Achievement Award," *Hot Docs Handbook 1998*. King had long argued that real-life events were intrinsically dramatic, and that actual characters and

plots often came in "perfect dramatic form." Allan King, "Portrait of a Woman," CBC *Times*, 13–19 August 1948: 5.

17 Eugene Hallman, vice-president and general manager, Network Broadcasting (English), "NFB Joey Smallwood Film," CBC Internal Memo, CBC National Archives Papers, RG41/series B-1-3/vol. 810/ film T-1-3-5; TV Information Programming: NFB 1969–73.

18 Judy Steed, "This Camera Shoots at Emotional Jugular," *Maclean's* 96 (5 September 1983), 53.

19 Ann Johnston, "Unemployment under Glass," *Maclean's* 96 (2 May 1983), 52. The corporation also had a hard time explaining the public service role of the shows. The CBC *Times*, for instance, noted that *Carole,* a 1966 vérité portrait of a Canadian teenager, consisted of "pictures looked at for their own sake without attempting to prove anything sociological" – though it then went on to claim (somewhat sociologically) that the subject's "slightly bohemian life is significantly free of youthful sick cults and poses." See "Camera West," CBC *Times* (2–8 July 1966): 13. Clearly, Canadian public broadcasters had a hard time condoning voyeurism for its own sake.

20 "Skid Row," CBC *Times* (6–13 January 1957): 5.

21 One "self-portrait of a real family" for *The Way It Is* (a predecessor of the famous 1974 PBS series *The Loud Family*) was based on over 35,000 feet of film, some of it captured by a CBC crew, but all of it shot with "devastating spontaneous candour," according to a press release of the time. See "Home Movies," CBC *Times* (30 August–5 September 1969): 15.

22 Steven Miller, "Sunday Night TV a Lot of Things, but Hardly Fun," *Maclean's* 80 (4 November 1967): 105.

23 Ibid.

24 Barbara Frum, "Television: The Social Problem of Women," *Saturday Night* 82 (June 1967): 38.

25 Douglas Leiterman, "You Can't Tell TV: Don't Peek," *Maclean's* (23 July 1966): 10.

26 Dingon, Jocelyn, "What a Nice Slum: Cue Camera One," *Saturday Night* (17 September 1966): 58.

27 Koch, *Inside Seven Days*, 66.

28 "Only when information itself is important enough to warrant broadcast" and never for "shock value or sensation." See CBC, *Journalistic Policy* (Ottawa: CBC 1971), 11.

29 Ibid., 27.

30 CTV, *Policy and Style Handbook* (Toronto: CTV 1975): 15.

31 Allan King, "Ironic Ethics," *Cinema Canada* 107 (December 1983): 24.

32 Michael Dorland, "Pawns of Experience," *Cinema Canada* 107 (December 1983): 24.

33 With the consent of its subjects, the program was shot over several months with a ceiling-angle video.

34 John Allemang, "Dirty Linen and the Ratings Game," *Globe and Mail*, 6 January 1999, D1; in short, while the vérité look came to have more of a hold than ever on entertainment television in the 1990s, the genre's status as a public service information form became increasingly uncertain.

35 Allan King, cited in "Allan King: Lifetime Achievement Award."

36 See John Fiske, *Understanding Popular Culture* (Boston: Unwin Hyman, 1989), 103–27.

37 Martin Knelman, "The Truth about TV Docs," *Financial Post*, 18 January 1997: 17.

38 Peter Goddard, "Warrendale: The Untold Story," *Toronto Star*, 17 January 1997: D3.

39 Knelman, "The Truth about TV Docs."

40 Kauffman, "Children of Our Time."

41 Joseph Morgenstern, "Allan King's Warrendale," *Cue*, 21 September 1968.

42 "Brave New Glimpse at Youth's Dark Side," *Sunday Times*, 17 September 1968.

43 "Yesterday's Children," *Financial Times* (London), 17 September 1968.

44 Kauffman, "Children of Our Times."

45 Greg Quill, "Banned Documentary Still Shines," *Toronto Star*, 22 January 1997.

46 Bill Nichols, *Blurred Boundaries* (Bloomington: Indiana University Press, 1994).

47 Mike Pelletier, "A Brutal Inside Look," *Ottawa Citizen*, 6 November 1967.

48 Mary Sheldon, "Allan King's Portrait of Misery," *Montreal Gazette*, 28 August 1967.

49 Pelletier, "A Brutal Look Inside."

50 Jean Baudrillard, *The Ecstasy of Communication* (New York: Semiotext(e)), 37.

51 "Spirit of '67," CBC *Times* (1–7 July 1967): 2–3.
52 Knowlton Nash, CBC Internal Memo, 16 September 1971, CBC
    National Public Archives Papers, RG41, series A-V-2/vol. 893/PG8-1-1,
    pt. 6, Public Affairs Programs: General Correspondence 1970–72.
53 CBC, *Annual Report* (1943–44): 17.
54 "Man at the Top: Explorations," CBC *Times* (28 September–
    4 October 1958): 3.
55 CBC National Conference, Outside Broadcasts Department,
    27 November–1 December 1961, Appendix D, 40, CBC
    National Public Archives Papers, RG41, series A-V-2/vol. 851/
    PG1-13, pt. 3.
56 Benedict Anderson, *Imagined Communities: Reflections on the
    Origin and Spread of Nationalism* (London: Verso, 1983).
57 "Crossing Canada," CBC *Times* (31 December – 6 January 1967):
    5. Rivers served as a trope in many of the Centennial shows, dem-
    onstrating Canada's geographic unity. *Canada 100*'s "River Stud-
    ies" (1967), for instance, showed how Canada's waterways had
    "affected and connected" the "lives of people past and present."
    See "Canada 100: River Studies," CBC *Times* (11–17 February
    1967): 3.
58 Ibid. Broadcasters had long attempted to imagine Canada in this
    way, thereby evoking a Canadian sense of community. In the
    1950s radio producers worked to overcome the anonymity of
    Canadian mass culture, the radio feature *Small Town* bringing
    audiences to Tottenham, Ontario, a town to which "passing
    motorists might pay little attention." It evoked an Ontario whose
    main streets a "tired traveller might regard as some fantastic belt
    carrying him on a never-ending circle through the same town again
    and again." See "Small Town," CBC *Times* (17–24 August 1952):
    3. In this view documentary broadcasts allowed Canadians to
    speak, record their difference and recuperate themselves as a com-
    munity – a community that may have been undermined by elec-
    tronic communications in the first place.
59 "Spirit of '67," CBC *Times* (1–7 July 1967): 2–3.
60 Benjamin Shelton, "A Nation's Dream Comes True," *Ottawa Jour-
    nal*, 16 September 1973. For an elaboration of this argument, see
    Paddy Scannell, "Public Service Broadcasting and Modern Life,"
    Media, Culture and Society 11, no. 12 (1989):135–66.
61 National history programs continue to assume this burden. For
    instance, the CBC's *Canada: A People's History* (2000) has

produced an extensive historical archive based mostly on oral history, *popularized* it by using journalists and dramatists rather than academics to tell the story, and *enacted* it by serving as an occasion for Canadians to "take stock of the Millennium" (Mark Starowicz, "Our Future Is Our Past," *Time*, 9 August 1999: 60–3). As critic John Allemang noted, "Canadians will mark the year 2000 in a characteristic way, with a big long educational documentary" (Allemang, "Major Television Event in Store," *Globe and Mail*, 5 June 1999). *The Canadians*, a four-hour CTV (1988) miniseries based on the recollections of *New York Times* reporter Andew Malcolm, similarly unearthed "surprising new facts" about Canada, offering them in a "popular acessible style" as part of a "24-karat television event" (Jennifer Wilson, "CTV Tells a National Story," 19 November 1988, *Ottawa Citizen*).

62 CBC, *Television Network Promotion*, no. 89 (12 February 1973): 1.

63 Ibid.

64 Ibid.

65 See below in this chapter concerning the representational claims of documentary journalism. For an account of NFB practices in this regard, see Marchessault, "Amateur Video and the Challenge for Change."

66 CBC, *Television Nework Promotion*, no. 89 (12 February 1973): 1.

67 John Urry, *Consuming Places* (London: Routledge, 1995).

68 CBC Program Proposal, "Canadian Civilization," undated, CBC National Archives Papers, RG41/series A-V-2/vol. 896/PG8-3/pt. 3; Program Archive Reports.

69 P.G.R. Campbell, general supervisor, Program Policy, CBC *Internal Memo*, 25 June 1971, CBC National Archives Papers, RG41/series A-V-2/vol. 896/PG8-3/pt. 3; Program Archive Reports.

70 Frank Penn, "CBC's 'Images of Canada' a Visual Feast," *Ottawa Citizen*, 17 February 1973.

71 L. Ian Macdonald, "Images of Canada: A Mirror in the Tube," *Montreal Gazette*, 17 February 1973.

72 Bill Musselwhite, "CBC's Fuzzy Image," *Calgary Herald*, 17 February 1973.

73 Lisa Hobbs, "Taking Stock of Canada," *Vancouver Sun*, 25 March 1973.

74 Bill Nichol, "Vincent Tovell's Visual Feast," *Vancouver Sun*, 21 March 1973.

75 CBC, *Annual Report* (1941–42): 10–11.

76 In the 1947–48 season, for instance, *In Search of Ourselves* offered a thirteen-part investigation of mental health with the help of the National Committee for Mental Hygiene. The project included pamphlets and study plans for listeners across the country. Documentary dramatizations were thus an integral part of educational discussion programs. See CBC, *Annual Report* (1950–51): 16.

77 Gilbert Seldes, *Writing for Television*, 187.

78 In a glowing review of Arthur Hailey's CBC docudrama *Flight into Danger* (1957), Thomas argued that the "mantle of the documentary ... may have fallen on the docudrama" (Alan Thomas,"On Television," *Food for Thought* [September–October 1957: 206]).

79 Alphonse Ouimet, "Sensationalism," CBC Internal Memo, 18 October 1963: 1, CBC National Public Archives Papers, RG41, Series A-V-2/vol. 897/PG8-1-1, pt. 1, Public Affairs Programs: Quest 1960–64.

80 J.C. McArthur, special program consultant, CBC Internal Memo, 6 January 1964: 2, CBC National Public Archives Papers, RG41, series A-V-2/vol. 897/PG8-1-1, pt. 1, Public Affairs Programs: Quest 1960–64.

81 Seth Feldman, "Docudrama Since 'The Tar Sands': What Now?": 16.

82 See, for instance, Miller, *Turn Up the Contrast*, 259; and Jeanette Slonowski, "Violations: The Boys of St Vincent," *Canadian Journal of Communication* 21 (1996): 365–79.

83 Ernest Dick, "History on Television," *Archivaria* 34 (Summer 1994): 215.

84 William Morgan, "Report of the CBC Ombudsman," in David J. Bercuson and S.F. Wise, *The Valour and the Horror Revisited*, 71.

85 William Morgan, "Comments on the 10 November Galafilm Report," in Bercuson and Wise, *The Valour and the Horror Revisited*, 97.

86 For an analysis of docudrama's formal features, see John Corner, *Television Form and Public Address* (London: Edward Arnold, 1995); and John Caughie, "Progressive Television and Documentary Drama," *Screen* 21, no. 3 (1980): 9–35.

87 Dick, "History on Television," 216.

88 Jeffrey Simpson, "CBC Series Marks Proud Page," *Globe and Mail*, 28 March 1998. Veteran officials were also given a right of reply following the 28 March 1992 airing of the program on CBC

Newsworld. If anything, CBC balance has been weighted in *favour* of conventional war histories. An early proposal for a "dramatic investigation" of World War I colonel Sam Hughes, for instance, was considered too controversial by the corporation in 1973, leading producer Martyn Burke to denounce CBC docudramas as "nothing but banal crap" (Martyn Burke, CBC Internal Memo, 4 July 1973, CBC National Archives Papers, RG 41/series B-1-5/ vol. 842/file334/pts.1-6; TV Information Programming: Tuesday Night 1969–7).

89 David Taras, "Struggles over the Valour and the Horror: Media Power and the Portrayal of War," *Canadian Journal of Political Science* 28, no. 4 (1995): 215–32.

90 Dick, "History on Television," 213.

91 Ibid., 203.

92 Koch, *Inside Seven Days*, 43.

93 "Newsmagazine/The Public Eye," CBC *Times* (12–18 November 1966): 3.

94 CBC, *Journalistic Policy Guide* (Ottawa: CBC 1982): 6–7.

95 John Kerr, head, Current Affairs, CBC Internal Memo, 26 March 1973, CBC National Archives Papers, RG 41/series B-1-3/vol. 811/ file T1-3-2-7/pt. 1; TV Information Programming: Current Affairs 1969–73.

96 Knowlton Nash, area head, Current Affairs, CBC Internal Memo, 3 May 1972, CBC National Archives Papers, RG 41/Series B-1-3/ vol. 811/file T1-3-2-7/pt. 1; TV Information Programming: Current Affairs 1969–73.

97 William Harcourt, executive producer, *Tuesday Night*, CBC Internal Memo, 19 November 1970 (CBC National Archives Papers, RG 41/series B-1-3/vol. 811/file T1-3-2-7/pt. 1; TV Information Programming: Current Affairs 1969–73.

98 Charles Jennings, assistant director of Programming, CBC Internal Memo, 29 April 1954, CBC National Archives Papers, RG 41/series A-V-2/vol. 893/PG8-1-1/pt. 2; Public Affairs Programs: General Correspondence 1939–61.

99 CBC National Conference Outside Broadcasts Department, Minutes, 27 November–1 December 1961, Appendix D: 16–17, CBC National Archives Papers, RG 41, series A-V-2, vol. 851, PG1-13, pt. 3. As one sales official noted, the "commercial possibilities of [shows like] *Camera Canada* would improve if our planning

was done further in advance ... If our sales people can go out with firm plans and even completed shows for a series, chances of selling a series will usually improve."

100 CBC, Internal Memo, "Controversial Programs Index," 25 April 1973, CBC National Archives Papers, RG 41, series A-V-2, vol. 894/file T1-3-2-7/pt. 7, TV Information Programming – Current Affairs 1972–74.

101 CBC, "News and Current Affairs Evaluation Process," Internal Memo, 24 January 1977, CBC National Archives Papers, RG 41, series A-V-2, vol. 895/file T1-3-2-7/pt. 8, TV Information Programming – Current Affairs 1974–77.

102 Ibid.

103 Robert Patchell, head, Current Affairs, CBC Internal Memo, 19 January 1971: 1, CBC National Archives Papers, RG 41, series A-V-2, vol. 894/file T1-3-2-7/pt. 6, TV Information Programming – Current Affairs 1970–72.

104 Knowlton Nash, "The fifth estate," CBC Internal Memo, 11 January 1974: 2, CBC National Archives Papers, RG 41, series A-V-2, vol. 894/file T1-3-2-7/pt. 7, TV Information Programming – Current Affairs 1972–74.

105 "The Nature of Things," CBC *Times* (17–23 December 1960): 7.

106 Martyn Burke, producer, CBC *Newsmagazine*, CBC Internal Memo, 15 February 1971, CBC National Archives Papers, RG 41, series A-V-2, vol. 894/file T1-3-2-7/pt. 6, TV Information Programming – Current Affairs 1970–72.

107 Knowlton Nash, *Prime Time at Ten* (Toronto: McClelland and Stewart, 1987): 39. At least five departments produced documentaries at the CBC in the early 1970s – News and Current Affairs; Agriculture and Resources; Arts, Science and Religion; Children's Programming; and Features and Entertainment. Their work often overlapped, leading to a good deal of friction, with the Children's department often pursuing adult themes, Current Affairs dealing with long-term issues, and Entertainment tackling actual events. But while programs in each area became ever more regulated by news and current affairs standards, journalistic hegemony was never absolute at the CBC.

108 CBC, Internal Memo, "Current Affairs Programming 1977–78," Toronto: CBC 1977: 2.

109 Ibid.

110 Ibid.

111 CBC, *Annual Report* (1989–90): 23.

112 W.A. Szemberg, "The Ugly Truth," *Saturday Night* (December 1994): 62–8. Launched in 1966 and originally modelled on CBC shows like *This Hour Has Seven Days* and *The Way It Is*, W5 adopted a more personalized and confrontational style. (See John Smither, "CTV Information Program Hits Hard," *Toronto Telegram*, 21 September 1968). Revamped in 1978, the program turned to "comprehensive reports" on social trends and institutions such as its two one-hour 1993 specials on Canada's public debt.

113 "A Novel Experiment," CBC *Times*, 5–11 September 1959, 4. These experiments were limited by the technologies of the day and a good deal of organizational in-fighting. Double-shooting for each network was too expensive, for instance, and "versioning" was usually impossible because early programs were only saved on final audiovisual prints rather than separate sound and image tracks. Network distrust was also a problem, with programmers often failing to agree on broadcast times that might avoid duplication in bilingual markets. To complicate matters even further, networks insisted their audiences would resist dubbed translations. In short, while "bilingual" documentaries were aired occasionally, and more frequently following the 1966 Royal Commission on Bilingualism, they remained "special events" on Canadian television.

114 Pierre Juneau, letter to Lister Sinclair, 19 December 1972, CBC National Archives Papers, RG41/series A-V-2/vol. 894/PG8-1-1/pt. 7; Public Affairs Programs: General Correspondence 1972–74.

115 Ken Black, assistant director, Television Information Programs, "Regional CBC Contributions to Television Information Programs," CBC Internal Memo, 10 April 1973, CBC National Archives Papers, RG41/series A-V-2/vol. 894/PG8-1-1/pt. 7; Public Affairs Programs: General Correspondence 1972–74.

116 Knowlton Nash, "Contributions to Television Information Programs," CBC Internal Memo, 10 April 1973, CBC National Archives Papers, RG41/series A-V-2/vol. 894/PG8-1-1/pt. 7; Public Affairs Programs: General Correspondence 1972–74.

117 John Kerr, head of TV Current Affairs, CBC Internal Memo, 2 April 1974, CBC National Archives Papers, RG41/series A-V-2/ vol. 894/PG8-1-1/pt. 7; Public Affairs Programs: General Correspondence 1972–74.

118 CBC, "Edmonton Producers Association," Internal Memo, 2 April
     1974, CBC National Archives Papers, RG41/series A-V-2/vol. 894/
     PG8-1-1/pt. 7; Public Affairs Programs: General Correspondence
     1972–74.
119 John Kerr, deputy director of News and Public Affairs, CBC Inter-
     nal Memo, 1 February 1969, CBC National Archives Papers, RG41/
     series A-V-2/vol. 894/PG8-1-1/pt. 4; Public Affairs Programs: Gen-
     eral Correspondence 1968–69.
120 "A Miserable Lampoon," *Halifax Chronicle-Herald*, 25 October
     1971.
121 Michael Stengold, "Toronto Strikes Again," *Ottawa Journal*,
     23 May 1974.
122 "Chamber Sending Protest to CBC," *Welland Evening Tribune*,
     20 March 1973.
123 Larry Grosnell, "Background to the 'Chemical Generation,'" CBC
     Internal Memo, 5 June 1973, CBC National Archives Papers,
     RG41/series A-V-2/vol. 894/PG8-1-1/pt. 7; Public Affairs Programs:
     General Correspondence 1972–74.
124 John Kerr, head of TV Current Affairs, "Area Heads Meeting,"
     CBC Internal Memo, 21 February 1973, CBC National Archives
     Papers, RG41/series A-V-2/vol. 894/PG8-1-1/pt. 7; Public Affairs
     Programs: General Correspondence 1972–74.
125 Ibid.
126 Nancy Shaw, "Cultural Democracy and Institutionalized Differ-
     ence," in Janine Marchessault, ed., *Mirror Machine: Video and
     Identity* (Toronto: YYZ Books, 1995), 26–34.
127 Janine Marchessault, "Amateur Video and the Challenge for
     Change," in Marchessault, *Mirror Machine*, 13–25.
128 F.R. Halhed, assistant supervisor, Outside Broadcasts, CBC Inter-
     nal Memo, 22 September 1961, CBC National Archives Papers,
     RG41/series A-V-2/vol. 852/PG1-18-1/pt. 1; Program Archives:
     General.
129 Harold Cardinal, president, Indian Association of Canada, letter to
     George Davidson, president, CBC, 16 April 1971, CBC National
     Archives Papers, RG41/series A-V-2/vol. 894/PG8-1-1/pt. 6; Public
     Affairs Programs: General Correspondence 1970–72.
130 Knowlton Nash, letter to Susie Huskie, Yellowknife, N.W.T.,
     11 January 1973, CBC National Archives Papers, RG41/series
     A-V-2/vol. 894/PG8-1-1/pt. 7; Public Affairs Programs: General
     Correspondence 1972–74.

131 Donna Lypchuk, "Ou sont les documentaires d'antan?" *Cinema Canada* (October 1989): 167.

132 John Kerr, head of TV Current Affairs, "Area Heads Meeting," CBC Internal Memo, 18 April 1973, CBC National Archives Papers, RG41/series A-V-2/vol. 894/PG8-1-1/pt. 7; Public Affairs Programs: General Correspondence 1972–74.

133 Knowlton Nash, CBC Internal Memo, 17 April 1973, CBC National Archives Papers, RG41/series A-V-2/vol. 894/PG8-1-1/pt. 7; Public Affairs Programs: General Correspondence 1972–74.

134 Peter Herrndorff, "Public Access TV: Issues and Implications," CBC Internal Memo, January 1972, CBC National Archives Papers, RG41/series A-V-2/vol. 894/PG8-1-1/pt. 7; Public Affairs Programs: General Correspondence 1972–74.

135 Knowlton Nash, "Immigration," CBC Internal Memo, 28 January 1974, CBC National Archives Papers, RG41/series A-V-2/vol. 894/PG8-1-1/pt. 7; Public Affairs Programs: General Correspondence 1972–74.

136 Herrndorff, "Public Access TV," 12.

137 Knowlton Nash, "Immigration," CBC Internal Memo, 28 January 1974.

138 Ibid.

139 Mark Czarnecki, "CBC's Daring New Gamble," *Maclean's*, 18 January 1982: 38. In 1981, as Czarnecki points out, the CBC's average audience share had dropped to just 20 per cent of English language viewers, down from 34 per cent in 1967. Even the traditionally loyal information audience had shrunk to under 600,000 weeknight viewers in 1980.

140 Ibid., 42.

141 "Take 30 1968," CBC *Times* (5–11 October 1968): 6–7.

142 Martin Knelman, "Their Finest Hour," *Saturday Night* (March 1983): 54.

143 Mark Starowicz, cited in Czarnecki, "CBC's Daring New Gamble," 40.

144 Steven Jones, ed., *Virtual Communities* (London and New York: Sage, 1996): 32.

145 Lucy Johnson, "A Bedtime Check-Up," *Winnipeg Free Press*, 17 September 1989.

146 Brian Melanson, "The End of the Road: CBC's Journal Signs Off," *Edmonton Journal*, 7 September 1991.

CHAPTER FIVE

1 Mary Ellen Armstrong, "Canada: A Case Study in Weaning," *RealScreen* 2, no. 9 (May 1999): 2.
2 Colin Hoskins, Stuart McFadyen, and Adam Finn, *Global Television and Film* (Oxford: Clarendon, 1997): 25.
3 Barri Cohen, "The Future of a Canadian Tradition," cited in Abbe Edelson, "Fest Plans Major Growth," *Playback* (3 May 1999): 23.
4 Armstrong, "Canada: A Case Study in Weaning."
5 The CPR, for instance, tried to attract European settlers with documentaries about various parts of the country. Producers were told to leave out all images of snow and Indians, though these were the pictures foreign audiences apparently wanted to see, and the pictures that ended up being featured in many of the films. (See Peter Morris, quoted in the 1997 CBC miniseries *Dawn of the Eye*, pt. 1, "Born Among Clowns.")
6 CRBC, *Interim Annual Report* (1933): 9.
7 "Intertel 1963," CBC *Times* (5–11 January 1963): 4.
8 Paul Attallah, "Canadian Television Exports: Into the Mainstream," in John Sinclair, Elizabeth Jacka and Stuart Cunningham, eds., *New Patterns in Global Television: Peripheral Vision* (Oxford: Oxford University Press 1996), 161–91.
9 Koch, *Inside Seven Days*, 20. Thus making the 1957 Fowler Report's recommendations for more commercial TV exports largely academic.
10 Nash, *Prime Time at Ten*, 81.
11 Paul Rotha, "Television and the Future of the Documentary," *Film Quarterly* 9 no. 2 (Summer 1955): 361–73.
12 Knowlton Nash to Norn Garriock, managing director, TV (English Services Division) CBC Internal Memo, 10 August 1971, CBC National Archives Papers, RG 41, series A-V-2, vol. 894/file T1-3-2-7/pt. 6, TV Information Programming – Current Affairs 1970–72.
13 Dean Walker, "Growing Export Market for Canadian Film and Television Productions," *Canadian Business*, (February 1960): 64–5.
14 Doug Nixon, CBC Public Affairs Producer, *Minutes*, National Conference Outside Broadcasts Department, 27 November–1 December 1961, 15, CBC National Archives Papers, RG 41, series A-V-2, vol. 851, PG1-13, pt. 3. A preference for home-grown information programming was deeply ingrained at the CBC, Knowlton Nash

insisting that the "real key to success in the struggle for more and better journalism on CBC television was not our foreign co-productions but what we produced ourselves in CBC News and Current Affairs" (Nash, *Prime Time at Ten*, 81).

15 Eric Koch, head of Arts, Science and Religion Television, "Information Programs," CBC Internal Memo, 30 December 1969, CBC National Archives Papers, RG 41, series A-V-2, vol. 851, PGI-13, pt. 3.

16 Knowlton Nash, CBC Internal Memo, 19 December 1973, CBC National Archives Papers, RG 41, series A-V-2, vol. 851, PGI-13, pt. 3.

17 Nash, *Prime Time at Ten*, 81.

18 "Export Sales," CBC Internal Memo, 17 June 1972, CBC National Archives Papers, RG 41, series A-V-2, vol. 894/File T1-3-2-7/pt. 6, TV Information Programming – Current Affairs 1970–72.

19 "Area Heads Meeting," CBC Internal Memo, 16 February 1972, CBC National Archives Papers, RG 41, series A-V-2, vol. 894/file T1-3-2-7/pt. 6, TV Information Programming – Current Affairs 1970–72.

20 A.H. McAfee, unit manager, Arts, Science and Religion, to A.H. Partridge, secretary-treasurer, "Intertel," 9 May 1972, CBC National Archives Papers, RG41/series B-1-3/vol. 965/T1-3-3-10/pt. 2, Intermag 1972–74). A 1972 proposal to boost documentary exports was similarly pitched as a "largely educational project" whose dollar returns would barely subsidize costs for overseas rights and the making of additional prints (Marcel Ouimet, "Tenth Decade: Further Uses," CBC Internal Memo, 3 November 1972: 1, CBC National Archives Papers, RG41/series B-1-3/vol. 840/file 295/pt. 2, Tenth Decade 1972–74).

21 Attallah, "Canadian Television Exports."

22 David Hogarth, "Canadian Communication Policy in a Global Age," in Colin Mooers et al., eds., *Restructuring and Resistance: Canadian Public Policy in an Age of Global Capitalism* (Toronto: Fernwood Press, 2000). See also Colin Hoskins and Stuart McFadyen, "Canadian Participation in International Co-Productions and Co-Ventures in Television Programming," *Canadian Journal of Communication*, 18 (Fall 1993): 219–36.

23 Geoffrey Gurd, "Canada," in A. Albarran and S. Chan-Olmsted, eds., *Global Media Economics* (Ames: Iowa State University Press, 1998).

24 Hoskins, McFadyen, and Finn, *Global Television and Film*, 17.

25 Robert McChesney and Edward S. Herman, *The Global Media* (London: Cassell, 1997), 19.

26 Kath Haley, "Documentary Climbs to New Heights," *Broadcasting and Cable* (3 November 1998): 46–50.

27 Barri Cohen, "The Future of a Canadian Tradition," cited in Abbe Edelson, "Fest Plans Major Growth," *Playback* (3 May 1999): 23.

28 Leo Rice-Barker, "Co-Pros in Canada: May the Best Deal-Maker Win," *RealScreen* 2, no. 9, (May 1999): 39.

29 Ibid., 31. The average budget for a one-hour Canadian co-production was Can$400,000–600,000 in 1998. Specialty channel license fees amounted to about Can$50,000–60,000 per show that year.

30 Statistics Canada, *Tabulations on Documentary 1998* (Financing – Foreign Investment): 3.

31 Andrew Freeson, "Social Issue Documentaries Hard Sell in Cannes," *New York Times*, 13 April 1998.

32 Kathy Haley, "Documentary Climbs to New Heights."

33 Nancy Hughes, "Latin Lovers," *Real Screen* 2, no. 9 (May 1999): 50–7.

34 Brad Stevenson, "Canadian TV Selling Out Worldwide," *Now* (19–26 February 1997): 12.

35 Doug Saunders, "Exporting Canadian Culture," *Globe and Mail*, 25 January 1997: C1.

36 Ibid.

37 Ibid.

38 Michael Kott, "Co-Productions in Full Swing," *Playback* (10 March 1997): 37. See also John Allemang's assertion that all Canadian television producers will "compromise their vision to meet the needs of their would-be partners ... producing product, something cheap and undemanding to plug a hole in a waiting schedule of a cable channel half-way around the world" (John Allemang, "Passing Judgement on TV's Best at Banff Festival," *Globe and Mail*, 16 June 1998: C2).

39 Statistics Canada, *Tabulations on Documentary 1998* (Financing – Foreign Investment): 3.

40 Hoskins and McFadyen, "Canadian Participation," 23.

41 Canadian Television Fund, *Documentary Programming Module 1999*: 2.

42 Doug Saunders, "New Rules for Canadian Content," *Globe and Mail*, 15 December 1998: A1.

43 Ibid.

44 Peter Allison, "Export Market for Doc Programs Heats Up," *Playback* (19 March 1997): 20.

45 John Panickar, Commissioning Editor, Discovery Channel, Hot Docs '98 Industry Conference, 20 March 1998.

46 Mary Ellen Armstrong, "Buyer Profile: National Geographic International," *RealScreen* (Fall 1998): 44.

47 Andy Fry, "Buyer Profiles: Animal Planet Europe," *RealScreen* (Fall 1998): 41.

48 M. Andreef, "Adventure Film Outfit Takes on TV," *Globe and Mail*, 15 March 1999: B7.

49 Simon During, "Popular Culture on a Global Scale: A Challenge for Cultural Studies?" *Critical Inquiry* 23 (Summer 1997): 809; and Roland Robertson, "Globalization or Glocalization?" *Journal of International Communication* 1, no. 1 (June 1994): 33–53.

50 Doug Saunders, "Exporting Canadian Culture."

51 Ibid.

52 Andreef, "Adventure Film Outfit Takes on TV."

53 Norma, Reveler, "Turning a Documentary into a World Marketing Venture," *Marketing Magazine* 103, no. 3 (20–27 July 1998): 8.

54 *Hot Docs '98 Handbook*: 45, 70.

55 Jody Berland, "Sounds, Image and Social Space: Music Video and Media Reconstruction," in Simon Frith, Andrew Goodwin, and Lawrence Grossberg, eds., *Sound and Vision: The Music Video Reader* (London and New York: Routledge, 1993): 37. Consider also the instrumental importance of place in nature documentaries. Industry observers believe the genre is a hot seller not because of any incipient hunger for local documentation but because of a demand for visual stimulation on the part of audiences and cheap programming on the part of broadcasters. See, for instance, Carl Mrozek, "Technology: Nature in High Definition," *RealScreen* (Summer/Fall 1998): 26–32.

56 "Intertel 1963," CBC *Times* (5–11 January 1963): 4.

57 Trina McQueen, cited in Doug Saunders, "Farewell to Big Canadian Dramas," *Globe and Mail*, 23 September 1999: C3.

58 Doug Saunders, "Documentary Makers Cast Wary Eye on the Future," *Globe and Mail*, 16 August 1997: C4.

59 Statistics Canada, *Tabulations on Documentary 1998* (Program Type), 1–2.

60 Malcolm Guy and Peter Wintonick, "Policy Notes," POV 1, no. 34 (Fall 1998): 9.
61 Canadian Television Fund, *Documentary Programming Module 1999*: 7 extra merit points are also awarded to firms that manage to secure network license fees above and beyond the minimum 15 per cent of their production budgets.
62 Doug Saunders, "Exporting Canadian Culture."
63 Tom Perlmutter, "Distress Signals," in Tony Dowmunt, ed., *Channels of Resistance* (London: BFI, 1993).
64 Leo Rice-Barker, "CoPros in Canada," 39.
65 Michael Kott, "Co-Productions in Full Swing," *Playback* (10 March 1998): 5.
66 Mark Starowicz, cited in Doug Saunders, "Documentary Makers Cast Wary Eye on the Future."
67 Ibid.
68 "Micro Meetings," *Hot Docs '98 Handbook*, 23. The scramble for funding also allows for undue government influence. For instance, White Pines Productions, which produced History Television's *Scattering of Seeds* series (1998), reportedly signed a contract with the Department of Citizenship and Immigration guaranteeing a "hopeful and optimistic" portrayal of Canadian immigration in exchange for production funds. John Allemang, "The Money Is the Message," *Globe and Mail*, 22 January 2000: R1, R4.
69 See Hogarth, "Communication Policy in a Global Age."
70 Stenderup, ed., *The European Documentary Sector* (Copenhagen: MEDIA, 1995).
71 "In Brief," *RealScreen* 2, no. 9 (May 1999): 6.
72 Mark Starowicz, cited in Merrily Weisbord, "The Banff TV Festival," POV (Summer/Fall 1997): 28.
73 Ibid.
74 CBC, *Rough Cuts Guidelines, 1999*: 1.
75 Mark Starowicz, cited in Doug Saunders, "Exporting Canadian Culture."
76 Ibid. See also Stevenson, "Canadian TV Selling Out Worldwide."
77 Anonymous, cited in Merrily Weisbord, "The Banff Television Festival," in POV 32 (Summer/Fall 1997): 29. The corporation still has its defenders. Commending a *fifth estate* story (2000) concerning Stephen Truscott, for instance, Rick Salutin has argued that "the CBC may be strapped for cash, but it retains a sense that this

kind of work is its purpose. In doing so it enriches our culture" ("I Am a Canadian ... Hero?" *Globe and Mail*, 14 April 2000: A12). In terms of funding as well, the CBC may fill a void by tackling programs that commercial broadcasters won't touch. Associated Producers' *The Selling of Innocents* (1996), for instance, was picked up by the American HBO Network only after it was screened at a Stockholm conference on child abuse, a conference sponsored in part by the CBC.

78 CBC, *Rough Cuts Guidelines 1999*: 1.

79 Martyn Burke, "'Burial Ground': Stillborn at the CBC," *Globe and Mail*, 24 August 1996: D2.

80 Susan Rayman, "Friend of the Auteur in Canada and Abroad: TVO's Rudy Buttignol," *RealScreen* 2, no. 9 (May 1999): 41.

81 Ibid., 45.

82 George C. Emerson, "The Channeler," *Toronto Life* (May 1997): 62.

83 Ibid., 63.

84 84) Steve Jonias, "Marshall's Message Reaches for the Sky," *Now* (17–23 May 1996): 35.

85 Emerson, "The Channeler," 62.

86 Catherine Mayer, "Animal Magnetism the Force in Doc Deals," *Playback* (10 March 1997): 21. Nature producers also work to "future-proof" their shows by avoiding topical references. See Carl Mrozek, "Technology: Nature in High Definition."

87 John Doyle, "Critical List," *Globe and Mail Broadcast Week*, 27 November 1999: 5.

88 Mayer, "Animal Magnetism the Force in Doc Deals."

89 Tertius, "Subjects and Objects," *Globe and Mail*, 28 December 1999: R2.

90 Norman Bolen, vice-president, History Television, cited in Gunther Bessen, "Docs in Canada," DOX: *Documentary Film Quarterly* (Spring 1998): 13. Documentary consultant John Marshall sums up the artistic impact of global versioning this way: "Whether you co-produce or pre-sell, you are probably going to have to make two or three different versions for each broadcaster because each will have their own requirements in terms of length and approach. It used to be that people thought a documentary was a sort of an untouchable œuvre" (Marshall, cited in Rice-Barker, "Co-Pros in Canada": 37).

91 Ibid.

92 Gunther Belsen, "Survey: Docs around the World," DOX: *Documentary Film Quarterly* (Fall 1997): 5–14.

93 Jennifer Hyde, CNN Commissioning Editor, Pitch Session, Hot Docs Festival, Toronto, 20 March 1998.

94 Amy Briamonte, A&E Commissioning Editor, Pitch Session, Hot Docs Festival, Toronto, 20 March 1998.

95 Jenn Kuszmyk, "Documall.com: Docs via E-Commerce," *RealScreen* 2 no. 9 (May 1999): 23–4.

96 Tom Johnson, "More than One Way to See 'Content,'" *RealScreen* 2 no. 9 (May 1999): 60. Digitalization also promises more back-up texts to help viewers make sense of the programs. According to Charles Humbard, vice-president and general manager of Discovery Communications, digitalized documentary programming will "make it much more plausible to realize multiple products for a project ... everything from DVD's to books." Cited in Carl Mrozek, "Technology: Nature in High Definition," *RealScreen* 2, no. 5 (Summer/Fall 1998): 26.

97 www.overcanada.com: 2.

98 Ibid.

99 John Allemang, "Fine Tuning," *Globe and Mail*, 9 October 1999: C4.

100 www.overcanada.com: 3.

101 Ibid.

102 Ibid.

103 Ibid.

CHAPTER SIX

1 And, I might add, from the margins of cultural studies. Here, the wholesale neglect of so-called "high cultural" forms is hardly more defensible than the dismissal of "popular culture" by an earlier generation of critical theorists. Documentary programming, like any genre, should neither be embraced nor rejected without a thorough contextual appraisal of its political-cultural effects in specific historical circumstances.

2 Tom Johnson, "More Than One Way to See 'Content.'"

3 Ingrid Volkmer, *News in the Global Public Sphere: A Study of CNN and Its Impact on Global Communication* (Luton: University of Luton Press, 1999).

4 Suzanne Craig, "Web Is Watching Them Work," *Globe and Mail*, 3 June 1998: B27.

5 Barry Glassner, "The Medium Must Not Deconstruct: A Postmodern Ethnography of USA *Today Television Show,* " *Media, Culture and Society* 13 (1991): 53–70.

6 Rabinowicz, *They Must Be Represented*.

7 Winston, *Claiming the Real*.

8 David Hogarth, "Agency and Structure in Cultural Production: A Case Study of Newswork at CBC Newsworld" (Concordia University, Montreal: Unpublished PHD dissertation, 1991).

9 John Corner and Kay Richardson, "Documentary Meanings and the Discourse of Interpretation," in John Corner, ed., *Documentary and the Mass Media* (London: Edward Arnold, 1986): 141–53. Goodwin similarly argues that the mixing of fact and fiction styles in reality TV has not led viewers to "tune out" or to seriously call into question televisual truth – leading him to rethink Marxist and Freudian explanations of television's power and pleasure in terms of "objectivity." See Andrew Goodwin, "Riding with Ambulances: Television and Its Uses," *Sight and Sound*, 31, no. 1 (1993): 26–9.

10 Rabinowicz, *They Must Be Represented*, 5.

11 Linda Williams, "Mirrors without Memories: Truth, History and the New Documentary," *Film Quarterly* 46, no. 3 (Spring 1994): 9–21.

12 Martyn Burke, cited in Doug Saunders, "Exporting Canadian Culture." See also Mark Starowicz's categorical assertion that a nation which "cannot produce its own documentaries about the Middle East, Europe, or South America … is relegated to the role of spectator" and "second-class world citizenship," in Starowicz, "Citizens of Video America: What Happened to Canadian Television in the Satellite Age," in Roger de la Garde, William Gilsdorf, and I. Weschellmann, eds., *Small Nation Big Neighbour* (London: John Libbey, 1993), 95.

13 Marshall McLuhan and Bruce Powers, "Epilogue: Canada as Counter-Environment," in *The Global Village* (New York: Oxford University Press, 1989), 147–66.

14 Felix Guattari, *Soft Subversions* (New York: Semiotext(e), 1992).

15 Anthony Giddens, *The Consequences of Modernity* (Stanford: Stanford University Press, 1990), 53.

16 John Tomlinson, "A Phenomenology of Globalization: Giddens on Global Modernity," *European Journal of Communication* 9, no. 2 (June 1994), 149–72.

17 David Morley and Kevin Robins, *Spaces of Identity: Global Media, Electronic Landscapes and Cultural Boundaries* (London and New York: Routledge, 1995).

18 Bryan Turner, "Postmodern Culture/Modern Citizens," in B. van Steenbergen, ed., *The Condition of Citizenship* (London and Newbury Park: Sage, 1994).

Index

Due Date	Date Returned
NOV 2 1 2007	NOV 2 0 2007
DEC 0 7 2007	NOV 2 5 2007
DEC 0 3 2011	NOV 2 1 2011
www.library.humber.ca	